For P.J.

With love, gratitude, and at least one incredulous high-five

Expecting

(A Year of Fixing Up and Breaking Down)

Expecting: A Year of Fixing Up and Breaking Down

First printing, June 2014

Copyright © 2014 Keely Flynn/Lollygag Blog

ISBN: 978-1-312-28359-6

Cover art by Dorrie McCarthy

Illustration by Emily Flynn

Contents

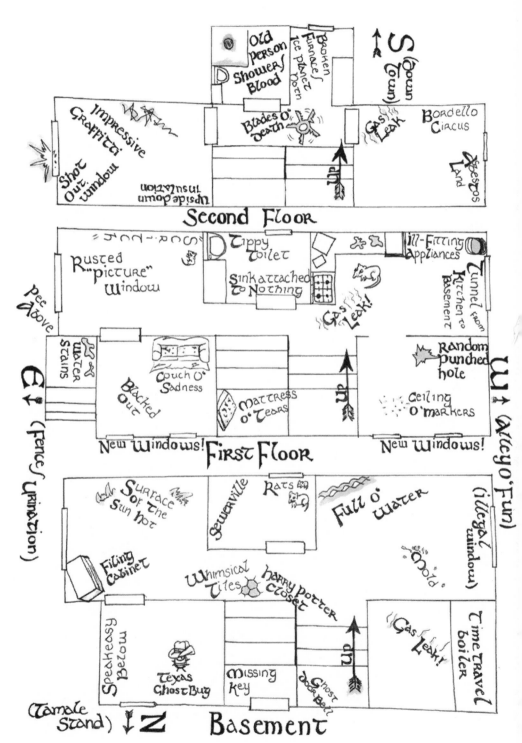

CHAPTER ONE

(Who is this girl and why does she blame everything on ghosts?)

I was alone in the house for the first time since we'd bought it. No realtors, no contractors, no paint-splattered husband to temper my fear of ghosts and unwise physical exertions. I walked around the upper floor of my new abode, surveying the rooms as my footsteps echoed throughout the house.

A friend who had just that day painted the nursery had needed to use no less than three coats of primer. But even with the layers and layers of Pale Sunshine, I could still see the primer's chalky streaks beneath. And underneath the thick primer, occasional bright stripes of red and blue shone through.

I looked at the doorless closet, decorated with graffiti and peeling black trim. The ceiling's soundproofing had ripped in parts, causing the small dot holes to become big dot holes. (And who had signed off on soundproofing the ceiling between the third floor and the attic crawlspace, anyway? Were the bats having a jam session?)

The windows still had bits of fuchsia peeking up from beneath bumpy black paint. We had covered up most of the really instructional graffiti and had done what we could for the fist-sized holes punched into the walls, but even after all of our work, the "nursery" still looked like a crack den from the '60s. Sponsored by a circus. So I cried. I wept for my poor future child, never to have a good night's sleep in this nightmare-inducing room.

I sobbed when I glanced across the hall and spied the master bedroom's window, still a casualty of some long ago gunplay, and which still needed major painting and sanding to tame the splintered chunks falling from the frame. I cried for the lack of doors on either of the bedrooms or the "master" bathroom. I bawled about the smell coming from somewhere in this cavernous, money-guzzling (yet cheaper than a new house!) home. I wailed because I was extremely tired, uncomfortably seven months pregnant, and indisputably alone- except for the suspected ghosts- on floors that, no matter how often I cleaned them, never seemed to lose their slight sheen of grime.

The crushing weight of the work left to do before our move-in, coupled with the knowledge that this whole drama was of our own doing since we had been *perfectly* happy in our old apartment, added another layer of grief to the mix. I couldn't for the life of me recall what had been so magical about this house when we were in the process of buying it. (Did it have impressive furniture? Had they employed some sort of Feng Shui wizard?) I cried for roughly ten minutes. Big, gulping, self-pitying cries, which soon turned into self-loathing due to the self-pity.

But that's a depressing way to start my story. And I'm rarely depressed, despite the few times that I've been seen (by ghosts or otherwise) crying at inanimate objects. So I'll give you some more crucial information about myself; stuff that will shed some light on who I am and how I ended up in a ramshackle home during my third trimester.

At the age of seven, I wanted to be a private detective.

I had an office set up in my bedroom closet- complete with sliding particle board doors- and a step stool upon which visitors could sit. Even though my rates were excellent, somehow the clients didn't come.

Still, it was my first dream job. Even better, it taught me that dream jobs don't always pay a ton. This was clutch, because my other dream jobs were (Famous) Actress, (Important) Writer, and (Well-Rested) Mom.

There was also a brief stint where I desperately wanted to be a mermaid, but I'm trying to keep it real, here.

The other game I played into the ground was House. I played House, Babies, and any incarnation therein for perhaps longer than was wise. My friends were trying out makeup and dance moves for their favorite New Kids On The Block songs, but I wanted to play with dolls. Or babies. Or dress up my younger twin sisters *as* dolls. We even had one really fun (for me) game called Baby Bears, where they would be my cubby bears and I would be their mama, stowing them safely underneath the dining room table for hibernation.

During "hibernation," sometimes I would go outside and ride my bike for roughly an hour.

My big sister would often play with me, too, stuff like Restauranteur and Improv Night and Roller Rink Concert Hall (*where* was the money in these ventures?), but she pretty much left me to my own devices when it came to Babies and House and Mauling The Younger Siblings. This suited me just fine. Turns out, the seven-years-younger crowd listened way better than the year-and-a-half-older bunch. And I was pretty specific.

I used to draw pictures too, of grand homes by the seashore. I'd sketch whimsical Victorians with wraparound porches, turret rooms with shutters flung open to the breeze, and tangled gardens of wildflowers. You know, the kind of houses that adults have?

Dollhouses were part of my bedroom's décor well into my adolescence. I didn't "play" with my houses, oh no. I decorated. I rearranged. I sloppily sewed miniature bedspreads and haphazardly glued handmade shutters.

I knew I'd own a house just like that someday (albeit slightly bigger), as long as I was a good person, worked hard, and, you know, grew up. Because everyone gets a house. In my smallish hometown of Pittsfield, Massachusetts, this was inevitably true. (Even though I knew in my heart of hearts, in order to be a successful writing detective and performing mother of a bear, I'd have to leave Pittsfield. At the time, the market was *not* good.)

I babysat for loads of families throughout high school, as well as for my remarkably resilient younger sisters. It was easy. It was great money. It was one of the first stepping stones to this crazy idea of being an Authority On Children. And with the minor exception of one of the twins who, while on my watch, fell out of a tree and impaled her arm on a branch, I considered myself a completely successful child caregiver.

After graduating from Hampshire College in the spring of '02, where I had honed the fine art of begging, arguing, and inventing my way through academia, I found the job market to be somewhat depressing. Even with my pretentious spelling of "theatre" as opposed to "theater" (signifying art form versus location), I knew I was in trouble. Here I was, ready to go with my mish-mash degree in writing, theatre, and writing *about* theatre, and I couldn't even get a job at my neighborhood Pizzeria Uno. (I applied seven separate times.)

A relative eventually suggested that I do some part-time nannying for a friend of hers while I waited for someone to hand me my dream job of editing/performing/getting paid (with the backup plan of detecting at a moment's notice). Aside from one sister's underarm scar and another sister's potentially very real fear of bears, I remembered that I had been quite good at the whole kiddo thing. I decided to go for it. At least until I found my "real" job.

I spent that summer caring for three little girls. And taking them to sibling rivalry therapy, having diamond jewelry steam-cleaned, ironing boxer shorts, and creating separate meals for each child. The hours could be long (I once had the girls' mother roll her eyes and ask *why* I had to make the train back to the city each night) and sometimes stressful (after walking trash out to the garage and finding the girls' father smoking a cigarette, he demanded that I not tell his four year-old. Uh, okay). I was also told that, while drawing pictures with the girls, I was hurting their creative confidence. (Since mine were better, obviously. To which I wanted to shout- I would *hope* that they were better, I just spent four years at an art school!)

But despite the similarities to The Nanny Diaries, I was quite smitten with the three gals and decided that, yes indeed, I could do this job while waiting for my Big Break.

So, when the summer was over and all of the girls were back in school, I moved to Chicago. I had planned to stay for a summer, maybe a year, and then either move to Los Angeles or back east and try New York. But, while I was in Chicago, I made the decision to really go for broke with this whole theatre thing, as I had been told that Chicago was (and is) one of the best places to work onstage.

I couldn't find a childcare job right away, so I answered an ad for waitressing at a distinctly terrible downtown bar and grill. After a few months of making a whopping thirty bucks a day during ten hour shifts (and *really* going for broke), I realized that it would be rather hard to hone my craft if a) I couldn't find time to audition, or b) I died of starvation. (At a restaurant! Now *that's* irony, Alanis Morrisette.)

I amped up my search for nanny positions and found a family in need of childcare for their newborn boy. And, when they moved a year later, I met another terrific family with yet another sweetheart of a baby boy. A third family was met during a serendipitous delayed flight back to Chicago and, besides having a darling baby girl, they also had a need for part time childcare. So then I had two families with whom to split a week. And when the second family moved, I met a fourth family, and a fifth who only wanted one day, and a sixth who needed the occasional nanny share. So that's how, nine years later, I found myself having cared for fifteen children, ranging in age from two weeks to eight years.

I soon considered myself a bit of an expert on all things Child. This, now that I look back on it, is a little daft, since I definitely had less than stellar moments as a nanny:

Like the time that I allowed a toddler to pee in a toilet *which I knew and promptly forgot* about how it had been disconnected from any actual water supply during a renovation. (Ever tried to remove all the liquid from a non-working toilet! It's really, really difficult!)

Or when I folded a load of my own laundry on top of an employer's bed (both of which were fully permissible things to do) and accidentally left a bra on the husband's side for the wife to find that evening. Nothing like insinuating that the nanny is hooking up with the Dad! (Also, why was I putting a bra through the dryer? That's incredibly bad for the shaping of said bra and that instance alone should have tipped me off that I knew absolutely nothing about anything.)

However, I *did* know that city kids love to play with woodchips in playlots (which they sadly believe to be indigenous to the area). And I knew for a fact that if I asked any child under the age of five to do or get anything, I had to become okay with the idea that it would take roughly twenty minutes for each task. And, when they eventually did return, after taking the longest and least straightforward route possible, they'd be wearing shoes made of Legos.

I also knew that there was a crazily strong dichotomy between mothers and nannies. I couldn't even begin to tell you why, but it's the sad truth. As soon as it comes out that you are *not* the mother of those kids; conversation over. I've even seen some just walk away mid-Ferber convo. At first it was strange, then hurtful, then par for the course.

But *why?* Ninety percent (a number I've completely just made up) of moms won't talk to nannies, and one hundred percent of nannies (for whom English is not their first language) wouldn't talk to *me*. The former had nothing to do with the latter, but it still stung. Maybe it's a transitory thing. The nanny could be gone from a family tomorrow, why bother trying to make playdates with someone whose authority may be completely obliterated by the next free museum day? Don't get me wrong: there are some awful nannies out there. Bunches sit there on their cell phones or chat with friends and completely ignore their children. (Guess what? Some mothers are guilty of that, too.) But to ignore all nannies out of hand? I mean, at least they got their jobs out of a process that involves applications and interviews. I've met *plenty* of mothers who were less qualified. And vice versa.

So, to sum up, I know superb mothers and stellar nannies. Also, I've met negligent moms and pathetic nannies. (See? *Expert*.)

I loved "my" kids deeply. They were way more than paychecks to me; they (and their parents, grandparents, and cousins) became family. But People In The Know (usually other parents) liked to inform me that, regardless of my close relationships with these children, it was Different Once You Had Your Own Kids.

Of course, I didn't believe them for two reasons; I was an *authority*, and I was in my twenties. That is not the best of combos for receiving Opinions.

Two years after I (temporarily) moved to Chicago, I found a guy who would soon stick my feet solidly into the Midwestern soil for the next decade, derailing any plans for following the Oregon Trail westbound (or, as my folks hoped, just coming *home* already).

P.J. and I met in the summer of 2004 during the first rehearsal for a late night comedy. I remember looking across the table at him and thinking, "This guy is going to be one of my best friends, I can just tell."

He recalls looking across the table at *me* and thinking, "She's really cute. So is the girl on her right. And the girl on her left as well. This is a cute cast."

There are people you meet in life whom you just kind of *look* at and realize- Wow, we're going to have a ton of fun together. When P.J. and I eventually got together, I could be sure of two things: One; that our careers in theatre pretty much guaranteed we'd be exceptionally good at not needing crazy amounts of money. And two; aside from that initial meeting, I knew that he'd always look at me like I was the only girl in the room.

The trips we took were epic and plentiful, as we were young, unfettered, and had no problem with cheap middle seats. We traveled well together, which is the ultimate litmus test for relationships. Lost luggage? Awful weather? Hip socket injuries after inadvisably walking from the Vatican to the southeast corner of Rome? Even though the last one was his fault, I found that there was still no one else with whom I'd rather *parlare*. Clad in hoodies, we took midnight bike rides to get junk food. We slept in our apartment's backyard to watch meteor showers (which is harder to do in the city than one might think, due to light pollution and/or concerned neighbors).

We were married on a day that looked a lot like that scene at the end of *Robin Hood, Prince Of Thieves*; pink petals floating through the air and a bunch of sun-dappled villagers. No royalty attended, but I'm pretty sure that everyone else did.

Our dating and honeymoon stage was a lot like a really good summer at sleepaway camp. (This is only conjecture since, as a youth, I had bad cases of both homesickness and sleepwalking. My only real knowledge of camp is from repeat viewings of *Meatballs* and *The Parent Trap*.)

Don't get me wrong, our relationship wasn't always a smooth sail. Sometimes it was a leaky canoe hurtling towards a waterfall. (During a hurricane with bursts of freakish hail.) P.J. possesses a really even temper and a tendency to keep things under wraps. Until. He. Is. Done. And I'm a sporadically explosive nit-picker, but then immediately feel better. Sometimes our fights would escalate due to the completely different level of "fight" we were both experiencing. (I believe that people should be angry when I'm angry and done when I'm done. I don't think I'm alone in this desire.)

We didn't worry that this inability to calmly disagree would rear its head- and bite us on the butt- during any of our future endeavors.

I'd found a really good partner for this new game of Grownup. Clearly, we knew what we were doing. Which is always what people say before fate comes along and kicks them in the teeth. I imagine the residents of Pompeii looked up at the morning sky and were just as smug about the day's weather.

We started talking "baby" early on in our relationship. We both come from large, close families, so we always knew we wanted to have kids. Lots of them. Someday. This is a very benign thing to "know," incidentally. Like, I knew I wanted walls with paint on them. Doesn't mean we should've gone to Home Depot and looked at paint samples for a first date. This did not stop us from debating names, number of kids (oh, at least eight), and where we'd all vacation every Labor Day. (Cape Cod. Or maybe Wisconsin.)

Sure, "someday" had a slight timeline. I knew I wanted to *think* about *talking* about starting a family (maybe) before I turned thirty. When we got married, this was three years off. Loads of time. So I started blog to chronicle our adventures. It became an outlet for my various writing ventures, but remained rather free form until the following year, which is what we refer to as *The Year That Everything Happened*. Then, the blog became a written record of the The Events; a time when a gal who liked things *just so* found that everything she knew about children was rather specific info tailored to other people's children, decided upon by their own parents. And the distinct realization that a home doesn't immediately become a place in which one would desire/ be able to inhabit, regardless of how many Martha

Stewart Livings and Real Simples one had previously inhaled.

The blog soon served as a cautionary tale, a How Not To guide for wannabe adults, and the direct result of hubris over all things Kid and Home. Those posts have been compiled into a neat little story of cosmic smack down and a tale of how a baby on paper is very different from the flesh and blood variety.

This is the story of my Non-Paper baby and how my (crumbling plaster) ceiling was permanently made my floor.

And how I wouldn't change a thing, even if I could.

Which is pretty clever to say, as people do not (to the best of my knowledge) possess this ability.

But I wouldn't.

CHAPTER TWO

(*And you thought THE MONEY PIT was fictitious!*)

Back when we were wide-eyed newlyweds, skipping along and holding hands, we'd chirp about our House of Dreams. It would have six bedrooms- no, seven! You've always wanted one of those stainless steel ranges, haven't you? And a kitchen island! Yeah, with doors that walk us straight out into our cabana!

To the future grandchildren of mine: I don't know much of this was covered in your fancy prep school/ hands-on hippie learning center- depends on which one us won out for your parents' education; but the Aughts were marked by a simply awful state of affairs, financially. But even with rock-bottom housing prices, we still weren't Bill and Melinda Gates (rich people).

We didn't stress about our lack of disposable funds. After all, it was A Buyer's Market, and we were in no hurry. Our sunny apartment in Chicago's Roscoe Village neighborhood suited us more than fine, and it even boasted a manicured backyard with its own strawberry patch and wild tiger lily garden. It was a skip away from some of the best brunch joints in Chicago- and, as everyone knows, the Young and Unfettereds love them some brunch. We were a mile and a half west of Wrigley Field and, even with my general apathy towards all things sporting, living that close to the Cubs meant that we were drowning in good/available bars.

Even though renting in a prime neighborhood doesn't exactly mean you can afford to *buy* in that same block, that didn't stop us from setting our bar way too high. Our new neighborhood would have to be even cooler than this one, we told ourselves. Yeah, and it would have to have a strawberry patch. There are standards and then there are *standards*.

We spent the fall and early winter looking at houses, condos, and McMansions, still just for kicks. The really opulent open houses were our favorites because it allowed us to play a new game called We're Very Wealthy.

Sometimes I'd tell the realtor that I was a writer. P.J. would nonchalantly offer up details about his latest project as a sound designer. Both of these occupations were things that we definitely did, but we sort of left out the supplementary jobs of nannying, software development, performing in completely humbling "comedy" revues, and cleaning the occasional kitchen. Those *workers* had no business being at an open house in Lincoln Square.

However, Keely the Writer and P.J. the Sound Designer would roll their eyes when shown a built-in wine fridge in the master bedroom (because, really, *again?*), debate who'd get possession of the home office/sixth bedroom, and whether or not granite countertops had been a little played out.

It was really fun, even though those homes and their owners didn't exactly believe in "the recession," and wouldn't entertain offers of less-than-asking price. For example, putting in a 275k bid for- say- a 2 million dollar house.

I'm sure the selling agents hated our guts.

It was during one of these fancy open houses where we met our first realtor. She was a very nice lady and didn't for a minute make us feel like we were wasting her time.

Which, to be fair, we totally were.

She was the listing agent for a gorgeous home right down the street from our Roscoe Village apartment. It was on a corner lot, boasted a magnolia tree, and was directly across the street from one of the best elementary schools in town.

It was also approximately six gazillion dollars.

She patiently showed us the home, asked me questions about my writing career (!), and asked us if we had ever worked with a realtor. We hadn't. She offered to drive us to see some of her other listings, if we'd like. (And we liked.) She asked us what kind of house we were looking for.

This, we told her, gesturing. We'd love one just like *this*. But maybe for under two hundred and fifty thousand?

To her credit, she did not laugh at us.

She took us to see places that were cute. Thimble-sized cute. And "cute" didn't belong in our House of Dreams search. "Cute" belonged to Apartmentville. Houses needed to have things like Space, Laundry Rooms, and Second Bathrooms.

And then there were those houses that were too awful to believe, yet too incredible not to mention.

There was one place on the Northwest side of Chicago that, sight unseen, seemed right up our alley. It was near a Brown line stop, on a tree-lined street, had a few bedrooms to fill with children, *and* boasted a backyard. Plus, it appeared that it would only need a little work. But then we saw it, and realized how much liberty can be taken with real estate listings.

Seeing any home at night is an exercise in using your imagination, but some are more trying than others. Our realtor, P.J., and I stood on a rickety porch and knocked, wondering why no lights had been left on for us. Nothing happened. We knocked again. A face appeared in the window, followed by a swoop of curtain. Furthering my notion that we had just stepped into a particularly Not Fun episode of Scooby-Doo, the creaky door slowly opened.

A man greeted us in Spanish. At least, we took his mumbled grunt as a greeting. We told him that we were supposed to see this house tonight. He yelled into the house to someone we couldn't quite see. The door closed. There was more yelling in Spanish between multiple parties.

Our realtor looked confused. As she checked her phone, I suggested to P.J. that maybe this was not the right time to view this property. That perhaps there was *no* right time to view this property. Because I had seen movies that began with this very opening sequence.

But P.J., manly man that he was, didn't fear angry men in dark houses. Besides, our realtor had convinced him that this was a Good Property. He took stock in those kinds of phrases, and I took stock in his opinions of people who said things like that. So we stayed.

The door opened again. The man gruffly nodded us in with his head. We rounded the corner into the living room and heard a voice exclaim, "Don't let them see me!"

What we *saw* was a queen-sized bed frame and bare mattress in the center of the room. On the bed was a rather obese elderly woman with a plate of fried chicken at her side. Before we could fully register what we were viewing, the man took a bed sheet and *threw it over the woman's head and body.*

"See the rest of the house?" Our reluctant tour guide shrugged a shoulder towards the kitchen.

Ever the diplomat, P.J. gave his brightest smile and threw an arm around my shoulders.

"We'd love to!"

The kitchen was in squalor. Cracked tiles had lumps of what I pretended were not human feces on them. P.J.'s foot went through one of the stairs. A small group of children followed us up to the second level- giggling at us the entire way- where we pointed at things and pretended that we could Really Do Something Cute With That. In actuality, we might have had to burn the place down twice to get the smell out. We didn't make an offer.

It was still slightly out of our price range.

We also saw a home we loved even more than the Fried Chicken House, somewhere we could definitely live. We said this to each other as we viewed the house from the street.

By this point, seeing the inside of a home was a bit of a luxury.

It looked kind of like a big rambly barn, with a large yard and tons of space on a Mayberryesque tree-lined street. Some neighbors walking by told us that it was the original homestead on the block. That sounded awfully fancy. A homestead! We were almost ready to sign.

It was a chilly autumn night when we finally got to see the inside of the house. The kind of night that would have been perfect in a Halloween flick, complete with a full moon and some ominous clouds. We didn't care. We were about to see inside our House of Dreams!

We waited (and waited) for someone to let us inside. We'd had an appointment, after all, and we were Good People, so we still had Faith In Humanity.

Our realtor, confused yet again, began making some calls. It was around this point that we wondered why she kept taking us to properties without owners, or why we couldn't seem to look at homes during daylight hours.

One hour and five phone calls later, she finally got a call

back from the owner. He was on his way home, just around the block, really. He'd be there in five minutes. Ten, tops.

Half an hour later; nothing. And did I mention that our realtor's young daughter was accompanying her mother on this late night venture? I found myself feeling guilty about keeping a second-grader out this late, concerned about what the heck we were going to see (if anything) inside this home at ten o'clock, and cold. I really felt rather cold.

Just as we were about to give up and call it a night/early morning, the front door opened. Apparently, someone had been home the entire time, but was not too big a fan of answering doorbells or phone calls. An elderly, shirtless man appeared in silhouette, gesturing us inside in silence. Once we were in the house, he returned to the attic and left us to tour the place.

This greeting deterred us not in the least, but I did wonder if Chicago's elderly were getting a commission from various realtors.

The house itself was nice. Once I trained my eye to overlook the two TV cabinets in the front room and more seating than would generally be required at a sporting event, I could tell that the room was a generous size with nice floors. Maybe nice-ish. One really had to squint extra hard to imagine what secrets the crammed floor was hiding. I chose to be optimistic, because I couldn't see or smell poop *anywhere*.

As we walked between the rooms, we noticed that the

floors felt a little creaky and perhaps looked a little lopsided. But the kitchen had recently been remodeled- in a style that seemed to suggest no update at all. We told ourselves that a newer ugly kitchen beat the heck out of an older ugly kitchen. (What had *happened* to our standards?) We walked up the skinny stairs to the second level, which featured four bedrooms. Two of them had sloppily been bisected by drywall, but we chose to admit that more bedrooms *are* better.

Our realtor had told us that the home was owned by a young family, but there were no sign of kid things anywhere. And it hadn't been cleared out in the staged way of much wealthier homes, either. After all, our first glimpse of the home was via Gramps in all his glory. There was one room adorned with graffiti and laundry piles on an unmade bed, but there was absolutely no indication that any kids had ever lived there.

As we climbed yet another skinny stairwell up to the third floor, P.J. ominously whispered to me, "Where are the *children*?"

The attic turned out to be spacious as well, so I can totally understand why the older gentleman cared for his living quarters so much. It featured a semi-finished room, a decently sized TV and mattress on the floor.

Although I did have another moment of concern over the bedding situation for our regional elderly. And these are the ones *with* houses!

Sadly, our dreams of owning this li'l piece of Americana were destroyed when the home was taken off the market a week later. I understand. It's got to be tough to sell a home when very few people are ever allowed inside.

It's important to note that, while our really great little apartment still continued to be everything we needed and wanted, we had completely become engulfed in the Winner Takes All mindset of house hunting. We couldn't *not* come away with a house at the end of this process. Chicago had become a gargantuan casino and these bizarrely kept homes were the penny slots from which we could not budge. (We apparently weren't allowed near the blackjack tables.)

There was the incredibly adorable house in Old Irving Park with picture-perfect details; gleaming hardwood, a lovingly restored kitchen, even a Zen garden in the manicured yard. The rear of the home was complete with a mature and shady oak, a curlicued wrought iron bench on stone pavers, and a bubbling fountain.

It also totaled a combined nine hundred square feet for both floors; the second floor of which, to enter, one needed to duck and turn sideways. And I'm barely five feet four inches. It was snug.

Or the new construction Victorian home in Logan Square that was absolutely gorgeous, the kind of home that people have in Home For The Holidays commercials. The dirt floor basement, however, did give us a momentary pause, as did the flimsy beams that seemed to be holding up the entire house. (I had been fully unprepared to realize that both old *and* new construction homes could be crappily built. It broke a smallish part of me, to tell the truth.)

And even though the mortgage would have been more than tight (bordering on suffocating), the offer from the builder to take out a separate loan from him as *well* as the bank was generous. As well as slightly shady.

A two-flat in a slightly industrial part of Avondale was up next. It had some promise, as we were given the option of renting out the other apartment (more moolah!) or keeping it for ourselves through a gut rehab (crazy amounts of space!) It was even across the street from a park. Sure, that street was so busy that our future kids would never, ever be able to cross it solo, but we could see a tree from the front door.

It also smelled really strongly of poop and the first floor seemed to be listing right into the backyard, but those two things were no longer deterrents.

By the time the body count of houses in our search numbered in the thirties, we had thrown out the list of mandatory "extras;" finished floors, completed countertops, and operable windows. We only spoke in full-on real estate ad copy. And we had also completely caved to whatever the realtor had decided to show us/whichever homes would allow us inside.

She brought us to another one on a frigid December night: tiny, sure, but "cute as a button". It had two small bedrooms on the first floor and a semi-finished attic with a narrow room attached ("perfect for a nursery or walk-in closet!") Even though the master bedroom was technically a barely insulated and would require us to go down a flight of stairs to the single bathroom, we were fairly excited to not have to clean our shoes after the first viewing.

This house boasted a decent yard, a door, some shrubs and a not-completely-ancient roof. It also possessed outdated cloth-wrapped wiring and an ungrounded whirlpool tub in that one bathroom. But at least it *had* a whirlpool tub!

There was a slanted sun porch off the back of the house, covered by a gigantic yellow nylon canopy which was held in place by rusted metal beams. The kitchen was floored with cracked linoleum and had cabinetry that my grandmother would've found too dated. The basement (which we started referring to as "the Lower Level"), had a crack in which you could sail a dinghy. The attic was partially done in faux wood paneling.

We decided that we loved it.

Feeling way too much like little kids, we made an offer that was ten percent under the asking price. I was of the opinion that we should pay what they wanted so that no one would feel the need to have any sort of confrontation. My coupon-adoring husband felt that ten percent was a deal *for the homeowner*. He reminded me that they were attempting to sell a cracked brick house that featured a death trap of a bathtub.

He was probably right.

Still, I stressed all throughout that night and the next day, wondering if we had hurt the owner's feelings, if someone else had made a better offer, and when was too soon to order new address labels.

Our offer was accepted, and I joyfully began to mentally decorate and plan out every inch of our dollhouse-like abode. I left the harder stuff to P.J.; though, to be fair, there was nothing easy about amending wood paneling and indoor/outdoor carpeting in the bedrooms. He would most likely disagree and attest that figuring out how to get a sun porch to quit falling into the backyard was a tougher task, not to mention all the work towards securing our financing. (We all have our strengths.)

These plans were short-lived. During the back and forth of contracts and agents and addendums, the owner backed out. We were completely floored, and not in a green and orange linoleum way. Devastated. Confused. More than a little angry. We were informed that this kind of thing happens all the time, which did *not make it any more right* in my martyred mind. We pursued it for a little while, but dropped it upon learning that the owner was in charge of Smith & Wesson training for the Chicago Police Department.

You win, Guy With All The Guns, you win.

We later found out that, on top of our annoying requests, the seller may have become peeved with us right around when our realtor failed to send our final contract back during the allotted eight day period. (She forgot.)

That, combined with the fact that a) the majority of houses we saw were completely crappy, b) the owners of those crappy houses never seemed to know that we were coming to see them, and c) *no one else viewed properties at night* caused us to break up with our realtor.

We still couldn't afford anything nice, but we promised ourselves we'd only see houses during the daytime hours. And they'd have floors, too. Floor and ceilings and *no more poop.* Not even ever.

We didn't entertain thoughts of giving up. After all, we were practically experts by now. We knew all manner of important house-hunting tips, like: Visualize yourself living in that house. What would I look like peeing on that toilet? Does it *have* a toilet?

Some might call that extreme optimism. Others might suggest insanity with a touch of vodka tonic. We preferred the term "savvy."

Drunkenly "savvy."

CHAPTER THREE

(We're what, now?)

During the housing search with our former realtor, we were still fancifully thinking about talking about starting a family. By the springtime, perhaps. Definitely by the summer. But apparently, even putting out tentative Baby Plans to the cosmos seems to be some incredibly powerful fate-taunting.

At the very end of February, we took a weekend trip to my husband's hometown of Cincinnati. We met our newest nephew, spent some great time with the fam, and found out that P.J.'s sis was expecting her first child. Fabulous news! I toasted this announcement with a glass[es] of wine. Serious revelry was had.

On the five hour drive home, I was feeling pretty poorly. This may have been due, as P.J. so helpfully suggested, to the glass[es] of wine that I had enjoyed the previous night. Still, after whining for a good half of that trip, he suggested we pick up a pregnancy test.

For the record, this was *not* how we usually dealt with feeling poorly.

During the three months prior to this test, my cycle had been a little late. Sometimes by a day, once by a couple of weeks. It became a joke. (Ha).

We bought an EPT and knew how this story would end.

Negative. Obviously. So we made a big, hilarious thing out of it. We walked in the freezing cold to our neighborhood Jewel-Osco, a three block walk roundtrip. We laughed about terrible names we'd give to our future-nonexistent-'cause-we-weren't-pregnant baby. Aggressively German names were on the table, as was the name Gunnar, after one of the dudes in the band Nelson.

And, to up the classiness of our evening, I suggested that whoever was *not* pregnant got to do a shot from the enormous bottle of Goldschlager we'd recently and rather dubiously been gifted. So, off the bathroom I went. Off to set up a game of Mario Kart Wii went P.J.

Incidentally, Mario Kart was how we dealt with any major decision or life-changing event. It got us through our engagement and more than one argument. Highly recommend it. On this night, however, it was supposed to be for plain ol' Kart fun. No issues. Just Toad n' Yoshi.

But, back to the bathroom.

There's no delicate way to phrase this; I peed on a stick. Left it on the sink. Chose an outfit for the next day's work. None of these were the activities of a Woman On The Edge of…Something. For clearly I wasn't.

A few minutes later I went back into the bathroom, that familiar panic bubble in my stomach. (What if I'm pregnant?) I ignored it. (I'm not.) But even though I knew there was *no way at all* I could be pregnant, I defy even an eighty year-old male to pee on that stick and not feel a moment's panic or count backwards on his fingers.

I checked the stick.

Saw a plus sign.

Blinked.

That was a definite, blue plus sign.

I checked the box in the trash. And it turns out that I had been correct in assuming "plus" meant "positive."

At that moment, I had my first ever out-of-body experience and laughed at the poor Pregnant Me standing directly below, holding a pee-covered stick.

Floaty Me and Stick-Holder Me meshed back together. I looked at the stick. I looked at my belly. Laughed.

Nothing was in the least bit funny.

Unsure of my own ability to walk all the way to the living room, I stopped by the dining room table and called into the living room. I could see P.J. in profile on the couch, intently playing Mario Kart. It was a pretty weighty moment; staring at him as he so blissfully played, certain that in a moment I was going to shatter that calm and potentially make him wet himself. (But really, why should I be the only one peeing?)

"Hey?"

"Hey."

'I think…we're going to have a baby."

That is actually what I said. I *knew*. Still, I said it. Like, if he disagreed or called my bluff: no baby.

He paused the game.

"What?"

"It was a plus sign. On the stick."

"That's- *fascinating*."

I've never seen a man walk into the bathroom that briskly. He didn't run, he didn't give an inch of this cool demeanor, he simply got where he was going very, very quickly.

"Huh. That sure is a plus sign."

After he finished checking my work he walked back to the couch in silence. Sat down. Resumed the game. Toad raced around the track, speeding willy-nilly into giant mushrooms and inappropriately placed farm animals.

I still hadn't moved from my announcement spot.

"Uh…"

"Yeah," P.J. spoke rather foggily at the screen. "I don't want you think that I'm anything but excited for this nor do I have anything but love for you *and* the baby. This…baby. But I'm just gonna need a little more time to process this, okay?"

That was fair.

"I kinda need to process, too."

He handed me the other Wii-mote.

No one drank any Goldschlager.

About seven weeks later, P.J. finally processed it. Apparently in Chicago, the doctors make you wait until the kid is teething before they schedule the initial ultrasound.

And it wasn't that P.J. didn't believe me- exactly- he just would prefer that this news come from a team of doctors, a police officer and my orthodontist. Despite the fact that everyone we spoke to mentioned there was no such thing as a false positive on a home pregnancy test (boy, *that* should be printed somewhere- is it?), he felt it would be better to wait until it was official before it was Official.

And there's nothing like seeing your lima bean of a child dance around your belly in an ultrasound, with your previously non-pale husband gripping your hand perhaps a little too tightly (FOR SUPPORT), to make things Official.

It was also a little unbelievable how fiercely and immediately we could love a lima bean.

Before the first ultrasound, we were able to time the whole deal back to around Valentine's Day. Which just about *killed* me. I mean- how cliché!

This meant that I took a pregnancy test when I was like an hour pregnant. Also, this meant that I was the kind of girl who began feeling ill as soon as she was an hour pregnant.

Don't get me wrong, I've always loved Valentine's Day. There's nothing fancier than red cellophane. That is a fact. And the brief moments of nausea were quite fitting, as I used to vomit with excitement before Valentine's Day classroom parties. (Never did make it to the end of the school day on any February 14th.)

On the Valentine's Day in question, I had made P.J. a collaged Valentine- one of my very best since I'd started making them in 1985- and gifted him a pair of warm gloves for his daily commute.

He bought me a flat screen TV.

It was clearly something on über sale that was meant for use by "us." Even so, since my name was on the tag, it was *for* me. And a flat screen TV was embarrassingly out of our gifting price range to each other. It made my gloves look a little pathetic.

I had to give the guy *something* else.

So, after the doctors convinced us [P.J.] that we were *definitely* pregnant, we told our close friends and family.

A fun little experiment to see if you have a perceptible drinking problem: decide to *not* tell friends and family about a pregnancy and simply refrain from drinking. If you're the casual "social drinker" that you perceive yourself to be, within one hour people will believe that you're either pregnant or dying.

It was actually fun to come clean. The shock value alone was a thrill. As we were among the first few of our friends to get pregnant, the overwhelming initial response was horror. This was followed closely by sympathy, then cautious congratulations.

Actual conversation:

"We're pregnant!"

"Oh my God. That's...good. Right? Are you going to keep it? Is Peej...okay? (It *is* P.J.'s, right?)"

"...Yes. To all of it. Yes."

Once people were able to jive with the idea that this married couple had a baby *on purpose* (kinda), they could get behind it. But this brought out even odder questions, like: "Well, you two certainly don't waste any time, do you?" Another favorite is, "Were you *trying*?"

These are both extraordinarily creepy things to say. Because the former makes it seem like the couple in question are just two little rabbits, barely waiting until they're alone to propagate their specific species. No one likes to be made to feel like a rabbit.

The other comment is perhaps even a little worse, because, come on. Even if they weren't trying, they're certainly not going to outwardly admit their own stupidity and carelessness! (Even though it's not always a matter of stupidity and/or carelessness, thankyouverymuch! Sometimes things just happen. A little earlier than expected!) Asking that question also paints a vivid picture of someone in a nightie, clutching a stopwatch. You know, actively "trying." See? Pretty bold image, isn't it?

Now quit picturing it. It's creepy.

Besides my twinges of slight seasickness, the only thing making it feel "real" for us was talking it to death. So we did, as obnoxiously as possible. Ooh whee, parenting was going to be fun! We'd make a nursery, get a stroller or something, and I'd have a cute little belly! We even uttered something along the lines of "Nothing will change. At least not for a few more months. If then!"

About a week after this incredibly stupid act of vocal hubris, those twinges ramped up to full-on Feeling Pregnant. Not in a glowy, nesty, Earth Mother way. It was more like the first hour you're awake after a crazy night of drinking. (Not me, though, Mom.) You *know* that the best thing to do would be to go back to sleep and pray you'd feel better in half a day, if only the floor would go back to horizontal.

It was like that all day. For about ten weeks.

"Oh, it's not that bad," Experienced Mothers would tell me. (More on *them* later.) This is an untruth. Constant nausea as the norm? For a good few weeks in there I was fairly certain that I was not pregnant, that I in fact had repeatedly ingested bad clams.

"Morning sickness, huh?" This is another Thing To Say, apparently. I have a theory that the term "morning sickness" was coined by men in the '40s and '50s, when husbands would kiss their deathly ill preggo wives goodbye in the morning and then go to work for seven hours. They'd have a three martini lunch, perhaps a happy hour cocktail, and then return home at eight or nine at night. Their wives would be fast asleep and the husbands would be too schnockered to acknowledge the bundles of abject misery sleeping beside them. Morning sickness, *ha*.

It got to the point where I could no longer get out of bed without having first placed a Triscuit into my mouth. This is true. No Triscuit equated feeling yukey on my way to the bathroom. And, while I had never had the strongest of bladders, I was now finding myself needing to pee at least three or four times a night. Nothing was even pressing on it. Yet. ("Just wait…" Oh, that amazing chorus from People Who Know.)

This is not to say that all pregnant women go through this awful imbalance of hormones and stomach flip-floppiness. Many have no first trimester symptoms. My older sister, for one. My mother, for two. I felt wonderfully special.

The constant feelings occurring between my throat and kneecaps left me a little surprised. Confused. Betrayed, even.

I dealt with this inability to sit upright by watching a crazy amount of television once I got home from work each day. I even coined the term Floppy Head for the feeling of being unable to support your incredibly heavy, dizzy, and puketacular head for even a second longer. Floppy Head struck at work, too. I knew it was a problem when one of my charges asked if we could play some Standing Up Games now.

Sure, I told her. In about three months.

I began working out. Apparently this is advised against, unless one is already a pretty regular athlete. And aside from religiously taking group abs classes at the Y in the months leading up to our wedding, I hadn't exactly been called an "athlete" since roughly senior year of high school. And it had been a pretty loose interpretation then, as well.

But I had a plan. And that plan involved looking svelte and magazine-ready for however long a pregnancy needed to be. (I was hoping to get it done in about six months.)

A friend of mine had recently begun teaching Pilates and needed some practice hours. And since *she* always looked svelte and magazine-ready (albeit sans pregnancy), I decided to give it a go.

It was deemed "gentle" enough by my doctor, and my friend even tailored a prenatal Pilates routine for us to do a couple of times a week at a Lincoln Park studio. Even with the pregnancy yucks, I began to feel physically fit.

It kinda made me wonder why I hadn't chosen to feel physically fit until I knew I was on the precipice of ballooning.

It was around this time that my husband began new rehearsals for a show that would go up in the spring. This meant that, two days into The Discovery, he began leaving me until roughly 11pm each night.

On a side note, the first sharing exercise that was done by the cast was won by P.J.'s bug-eyed announcement that his wife was pregnant. Kinda. Very recently. But "shh." This was met with the expected "*whaaat*" of his fellow actors, akin to if he had just proclaimed that, over the weekend, he had learned how to fly.

Regardless of how supportive of his acting career I was, or how terrific this company was, I could not believe how the entirety of the theatre community was conspiring against me during my pregnancy.

So I turned to salt. Not like Lot's wife, but rather I began a torrid, ten month affair with the substance. (Did you know pregnancies lasted for ten months as opposed to nine? *Threw me, too*!)

Salt understood me, spooned me as I face-planted on the couch, and quelled my bizarre cravings and queasiness. Chips, cured meats, and anything in brine *at all* were the only ways my stomach would quit the constant elevator-dropping going on in my abdomen.

"Like butterflies," I was asked? Yeah. Like butterflies. On steroids. With a point to prove to your kidneys.

My incredibly thoughtful aunt had, the month prior, sent a box of humongous lemons from her tree in Arizona. She couldn't possibly have known that fresh squeezed lemonade (made nightly by P.J., desperate to rack up points to counteract his abandonment) would be the beverage of choice during this trimester. Most nights I'd down a pitcher, easy. Salt and citric acid kept my stomach nicely preserved during this bizarre time.

Shortly after these two gateway drugs, I became better acquainted with my friend Taco. I'd always counted the crunchy-shelled taco as one of my very best dinner pals, but now he was a back alley meet-up, a rabid, four times a week obsession. His sidekick Red Onion became a shiny star in my universe, later trading up to leading man material. Meals that called for a slice of onions would get two or three helpings, and eventually we wouldn't even need the pretense of the rest of the meal.

To completely rip a page from the Big Book of Clichés, my main man Pickles joined my edible love triangle. (Quadrangle?) I was so thoroughly ashamed of myself- what was next, ice cream on toast? Grapes dipped in barbecue sauce?

But with the cravings came the Aversions; things usually so bland as to be unnoticeable in my food spectrum were now simply intolerable. For example, the chicken. The chicken has done nothing but love me; serving as a demure hostess in the

Armenian cuisine of my youth, grilled up with expertise by my Dad to signal the start of summer, or playing the lead in my parents' Cajun Alfredo sauce. Suddenly, I wanted him out. I didn't want to see The Chicken, smell him, or know he was in the freezer. Dumpsville, Population: One box of Perdue skinless breasts, sittin' on the curb.

Then came the stuff I could no longer enjoy. Sushi! Red wine! (Or any color, really.) Deli meats; which didn't really affect my diet all that much, but whoo boy, telling a pregnant lady she can't have something? You'd think Black Forest ham and I were the Montague and Capulet kids. And then there was the coffee thing. The day I discovered my pregnancy, I had just enjoyed my eighth cup of (small) coffee. I did this coffee overkill sometimes when working on a new play or during rehearsals. My doctor patiently informed me that yes, coffee was fine, but perhaps I shouldn't be having *that* much. We settled on three. (Guess what? Those Starbucks servings count as two! Sure, the word 'tall' is right there, but still!) My coffee intake had just been slashed to nearly nothing, and I had never needed it more. Floppy head? Nausea? Now I actually had to *rest* to deal with these things.

Still, I didn't think the new food restrictions would affect me all that much; I'd always prided myself on being rather healthy. Then I underwent the preggo detox and tossed out excessive starches, processed food, and alcohol. Turns out, in my twenties I was the equivalent of a junkie behind the A&P.

Also, strangely enough, my prior sensitivity to chili peppers seemed to go away overnight. Spicy foods used to cause hives and swollen lips, and not in a hot, Botox way, either. More like: Wow! Has someone recently swatted you square in the kisser with a toaster oven? But seemingly in an instant, curry was harmless and just really good.

This led me to believe that I now possessed super powers. Of course, I couldn't do anything about the spleen-shattering nausea or the apparent narcolepsy, but I could eat Indian food. And that was pretty cool.

But that was it insofar as the "pros" category went. I was a mess. I knew I was a mess. So did my family and pals, but they tolerated me. I'm not quite sure how I wasn't shoved off a pier during these months. I was a whiny whiner and I suddenly couldn't deal with my own pregnancy. Not the reality of the baby, mind you; that eyeball-popping Asphyxiation Fest was still a few months off. But the actual aches and pains of creating a new life were debilitating.

It was really weird. I had always wanted a baby (someday!) and had a rough idea of what to "do" with a baby, but the reality of pregnancy had never really entered my mind.

Oh, and it got real.

Before, I had never had much in the way of hips. Puberty

at twenty-nine surprised me slightly. It seemed that overnight, thumbs began digging into my hip sockets and shoving outwards. For the baby! People loved saying that. (I cannot stress enough how much people love talking at pregnant women.)

Another good friend of mine would occasionally accompany me in these tear-stained, salt-induced Queasy Fests. Like any pal with mad massage therapy skills, she'd help me order way too much food, tolerate requests to rub my aching everything, and let me pretend to watch a movie; when in actuality I was about to fall asleep on her shoulder and cover her with drool. We got part way through *Wall-E*, once. I think I cried and passed out before Eve landed. That's like ten minutes in.

I decided to educate myself about every detail of this lima bean, whom we nicknamed "Bitsy," and later "Bitsy Baby Pickles" (as "Li'l Bitsy Onions" seemed a bit too carny.) My oldest sister, the one of No Symptoms fame, gave us a great book that detailed what the kiddo bean was doing on any given day. Every week we'd read a new chapter on what the Bits was doing, learning, feeling and growing. It became the new crack (granted, we'd never had an "old" crack) to see what the baby had that he or she hadn't possessed just a few days prior. The day we realized the baby had toenails? Crazy jubilation. High fives, even. Look what we *did*!

This helped to abate the queasiness. Okay, not all that much. But it was nice to focus on the "end result." The "prize." (People also really like to speak in quotation marks at pregnant women.)

And, in case anyone's worried about a dearth of baby websites on the internet, you don't have a thing to fret about. My simultaneously pregnant sister-in-law and I joined various sites and received even more updates about every single thing that was occurring, as well as even more stuff to worry about. There were also groups to join of moms-to be who have similar due dates and are even crazier than you.

This becomes helpful, trust me.

Pregnancy sites love to describe your child's various stages as food; the size of a Crenshaw melon, for example, or a loaf of bread. The initial update informed me that my fetus was the size of a poppyseed. (That is ridiculously small. Also ridiculously impressive that something of that size could drop me like a WWE wrestler.) I'm not so sure, however, that the food-comparison choice is a correct one. Initially, telling someone that their child is the size of a peanut could send her running to the bathroom. Later in the pregnancy, comparing him to a pot roast could send her running to the kitchen.

Which would indirectly cause a weight gain of around forty pounds. For example.

I started a short-lived campaign to change these sizes to

actual objects: a sand pail, some nail clippers, a neck pillow…

I had to give it up. I was way too tired.

At the end of March, we flew to Los Angeles. And if you're wondering if it perhaps wasn't a wise idea to fly a bundle of hormones and nausea across the country, you'd be correct. I probably wasn't the most fun thing P.J. has ever had the pleasure of sitting next to for five hours. But when it came down to it, I had to make the choice between staying (and whining) at home or being nauseous in California while living out a major dream.

Earlier in the year, I had won an international novella competition for the twentieth anniversary of the TV series *Quantum Leap*. The awards ceremony was to take place at a fan convention. And the winner would have a copy of their book handed to creator/producer Donald Bellisario, producer/writer Deborah Pratt, and- one of my favorite people in the history of ever- actor Scott Bakula.

This is all one thousand percent true.

I won a *Quantum Leap* fan fiction contest and was due to meet my idol. There was no way that pregnancy was going to rob me of this once in a lifetime foray into Nerd Glory.

Our original itinerary (booked when I was so much younger, so much less seasick), included a weekend in L.A. and then a drive up to Napa for some serious vineyard damage.

Obviously, some of this planning needed to be tweaked.

We spent a truly glorious weekend in Los Angeles. I did all sorts of things that would have made my nine year-old self's heart skip a dorky beat.

I participated on a *Quantum Leap* trivia panel and got totally schooled by people who knew every detail about every minor character, ever, including one girl who knew Sam Beckett's (a fictitious character, mind you) social security number.

But as P.J. consoled me, sometimes it's okay to be the least geeky person at a sci-fi/fantasy convention.

There was an opening ceremony event and dance party. And even with my midsection straining through my pre-pregnancy layered clothing (darn it!), P.J. and I were still the most over-dressed people there. Because there were totally people sitting on folding chairs, clad in sweatpants.

I received a medal- *a medal-* for my award-winning novella. There was applause. I thanked Donald Bellisario for creating my favorite series ever. ("Uh, you're welcome.") Deborah Pratt, whom I had totally befriended and embarrassed myself in front of earlier in the day, hugged me in congratulations.

And then I shook the hand of my idol, Mr. Scott Bakula himself, and babbled something incoherent. P.J. assures me that I did not drool. We hugged. There was photographic evidence.

My mind and heart and soul gasped with happiness and I informed P.J. that I was ready to return home. I had done everything I could ever possibly do in this life.

P.J. kindly told me that we had four more days and plenty of reservations still to go in California, not to mention a few other plans in the works for the next year.

So we drove up Highway 1. Sure, there were quicker ways to get to Monterey, the second stop on our trip, but none of those other (nighttime, pitch black) routes featured sheer cliff drops that would make even a *non*-pregnant woman hurl.

As P.J. let loose his inner Hell's Angel and screamed "This is wild!" into the windy darkness of the twisting roads, I apologized to our unborn baby. It sure would've been nice to have been a Mom, I whispered to my lurching stomach, reacting with full-body winces every time I spied oncoming traffic.

Once in Monterey, we went to the Aquarium where I encountered the otters. This was a defining moment in my pregnancy, early on though it was.

The otters were playful and having a good ol' time showing off for the cooing visitors. I took over forty glamour shots. (Forty shots of *otters*.) The rest of the aquarium visit was fun- the glowing jellyfish tanks, the balcony breezes coming off of the bay- but I couldn't get the otters out of my head. Their cuteness had permeated my entire being. I was still feeling a little precarious, what with the recent cliff drive and the even more recent hormonal spike, and I wasn't sure if I could handle leaving the aquarium without seeing the otters one more time. (It bears noting that, while I've always *liked* the otter as an animal, my feelings had never even come close to approaching this middle school crush mindset.)

So we saw the otters again. We said goodbye yet again and made our way back to the street through the gift shop.

And there, on an unassuming shelf, was a cuddly pile of miniature plush otters. They were each clutching a tiny velvet baby blanket embroidered with the phrase "Baby's 1st Otter."

Never mind that it looked more like "ist" than "1st." Never mind that "Baby" was in no real danger of having a "2nd" or "3rd" otter. And never mind that P.J. might have found the stuffed animal kind of odd looking.

I cried. Actually, I bawled in shame, with poorly suppressed tears that made me grab my ribcage and belly because my lungs hurt and I was afraid that I'd vomit all over this nice gift shop floor.

I was already so incredibly in love with this otter for my baby and was already so incredibly sad that I could *not* (since I knew my husband and his naysaying ways) take home the whole pile of 1st Otters.

We bought one. I named him Otto.

I kept him in my bag for the rest of the day, occasionally taking him out and welling up with utter (otter?) emotion.

I'm pretty sure P.J. felt that he dodged a big ol' Otter Bullet with the purchase of the one otter lovie as opposed to, say, an actual otter.

Eventually, we made it all the way up to San Francisco (our alternate trip for Napa) and proceeded to do all sorts of nausea-inducing things:

We took the BART train three times in an hour (from the airport where we dropped off our rental and back and then into the city again) in pursuit of P.J.'s lost sunglasses. Never did find the darned things, ha ha! Enjoy your stay!

We dined in the city's oldest Italian restaurant where (as P.J. is quick to point out) I ordered the most expensive item on the menu and then proceeded to eat one bite of veal before deciding I might never eat again. (I spent the rest of the meal in tears, due to extreme stomach floppiness and the knowledge that I had wronged my extremely disappointed husband.)

We took the rather choppy Alcatraz ferry. Twice. (On the first trip, I was clutching the leftover veal and some dinner rolls, attempting to make amends for the previous night's wastefulness with my questionable breakfast choice.)

And we took a bicycle built for two clear over the Golden Gate Bridge into Sausalito.

Anyone who tells you how whimsical that can be is a big frickin' liar. The balance required (not to mention trust) to hurl two bodies uphill, across a really, *really* windy and high up place and then to zoom downhill, is downright Cirque du Soleil. Add a queasy scaredy cat to the mix as well as her schedule-happy husband, and you've got a recipe for a great couple's outing.

Flying back to Chicago and hauling our stuff home seemed rather relaxing after our vacation.

Once back from La La Land, I found myself in the region of Nothing Fitsville, so I had my first foray into shopping for maternity clothing.

There's this fun idea that once a woman gets pregnant, she suddenly wants to clad herself in either a) bold colors and patterns that scream I Am Getting Larger, or b) really cutesy images. Sure, I'm having an infant. I'd rather not look like one.

And then there was the issue of bras. Suddenly, nothing fit. Did you know that, during pregnancy, a woman's ribcage actually expands? I sure as heck didn't!

I had started out with a fairly normal ribcage/cup size ratio (one that, naturally, I used to complain about during my *absolutely issue-free twenties*) but a few months into the pregnancy things started to, well, grow.

"Don't buy any new bras yet," people would caution. "You're just gonna get bigger. And *bigger.*"

So what was I supposed to do? Obviously I wasn't about to plunk down twenty or thirty bucks for a "good" bra every month. (Isn't it criminal how expensive a good bra is? And forget cheaping it out. Sure, you can get one for about six bucks. And later you can lament to your chiropractor how you thought wearing bra straps the consistency of silly string was a decent idea.) But the idea of layering two built-in bra tanks and pretending that it didn't leave me gasping like a fish out of water and kept anything even *near* the anatomical neighborhood where they were supposed to live wasn't working for me, either.

And there's this whole, ugly debate about soft cup versus underwire during pregnancy and nursing, and there are no winners. None. Soft cups reduce the chance of blocked ducts and mastitis, but underwire provides lift, which eases pressure on one's back and lessens the stretch marks due to gravity.

Whatever. At this point, I would have accepted stretch marks on my face if I could've just found a bra that fit and a cot on which to rest.

I headed to Target and their maternity section. Maybe there existed a middle ground between cheap asphyxiation and undergarments pricey enough to be framed as wall art. But there were no bras there. Weird, huh? That's definitely a "maternal" item of clothing, I thought to myself. I asked a team member, or whatever it is that they're called (don't get me wrong, I adore Target, but their vacant stare method of assistance can leave a tad to be desired) and was promptly informed that nursing bras weren't in maternity. I inquired as to where they might be. Shrugging, the gal actually pointed me in the direction of the

Photo lab. I felt slightly dirty, but I asked the photo kid where I could possibly find a nursing bra. Or a tank. (Or a large bed sheet. I just really wanted to go home.)

He sent me to Lingerie. Go figure. However, once there, it took me a good ten minutes to find the nursing section. As it turns out, the best place for items befitting a newly bulbous woman is behind a display of socks, turned sideways against one of those huge, rectangular support posts. I actually had to turn and reach my arm to get them out.

And they didn't have my size.

Which is fair, because at this point, I didn't even *have* a size.

Then I headed to Macy's. This was a big deal, and one I had to keep kinda hush-hush. For I reside in Chicago. And in Chicago, Macy's is only cool if you call it by its real name: Marshall Field's. Which no longer exists because of the big ol' Macy's in its former building. And that's the problem. But after a while, regardless of how stalwart one is, you just need to go to a store where people speak eloquently and treat you like you're not ruining their day.

Upon entering this maternity section, I could tell that this would be different. Better. Inspiring. Safe. A grandmotherly woman approached me, correctly guessed how far along I was, estimated a few types and sizes of bras, and gently whisked me into a room for a personal, topless fitting (for which I was not immediately prepared) and proceeded to hand me two perfect bras. Just like that. And they fit.

For now.

I was now well-equipped with decent maternity wear and salty snacks, and felt ready to carry out the rest of my gestational sentence in relative comfort. But I still had to get places. And that would involve public transit.

The buses and trains in Chicago have a kind recorded message requesting people to give up their seats for the elderly, the handicapped, and expectant mothers. This is a great suggestion. It is also just about as effective as requesting drunken Cubs fans to not puke on the seats. (Read: *not* effective.)

Once I started to show a little bit, I naturally assumed that folks would hop up and insist on my taking of their seats. And by "showing a little bit," I mean that I consistently appeared about three months ahead of my pregnancy schedule. I popped early and kept on growing. When they didn't notice or care, I would poke out the ol' belly and place a hand on the side of it. This is, of course, the universal sign for "pregnant."

If ever you're not sure if a woman is with child or just a little chunky, watch for the hand. Hefty gals rarely caress the tummy.

I didn't feel bad in the *least* for using the pregnancy this way. Of course, my innate fear of confrontation refused to let me just *ask* for a darned seat. I didn't want to seem needy. And there's nothing needier than a chick trying not to appear needy. So I began willing people to get up with my mind. And baleful looks. And deep sighs.

Eventually, someone would capitulate.

It was usually an elderly man with crutches. (I wouldn't take the seat.)

And truly, I had never needed priority seating more than when I was navigating the extreme fatigue, weird aches, and unsettled stomach of the newly pregnant. Although, perhaps women in the first trimester should avoid public transit at all costs. Especially during rush hour. And on game days. There's just something about the combo of punctuated motion and the scent of stale beer to really make you wish you'd gone for the family size box of Triscuits.

During one especially crazy rush hour/Cubs day mash-up, I overhead two (seated) teenaged boys respond immediately to each other after hearing the recorded message, "Why would a pregnant person need to sit?" "Yeah. Fat ass."

I kept the rage so tightly bottled that I almost popped an eyeball. I think I cried a little. But, since I was pressed tightly against a germy handrail, my sobs were muffled and my tears were merely a drop in the endless sea of bodily fluids present on the ol' 152.

We had a second ultrasound at the twenty week mark. This was even better than the first one, which pretty much only served to prove that something was going on in there. *This* one was fun. Everyone fully acknowledged that, yes, there definitely was a wriggling loaf of bread making itself comfy; let's just check it out, shall we? I loved getting to see the kiddo, even though the methods they used early on to see the baby were rather uncomfortable. (I'll leave this one as a pleasant surprise for expectant mothers. Okay, here's a hint: it's internal. And *really* cold. And slightly pornographic. I've said too much. Enjoy!)

We couldn't wait to learn more about this kid. Not the gender- no sir- since we were part of a confusing portion of the population who wished to be surprised on delivery day.

"How do you know how to *decorate* for the baby?" This was a common and bewildered question presented to us.

Uh, like it's a room for a baby. It's not a surprise Sweet 16 party; the kid will *not* be disappointed in us for at least another decade and a half. Besides, once someone has a girl or a boy (one or the other is pretty much guaranteed), the new family will get positively inundated with pink or blue paraphernalia. So, there's plenty of time for that hurricane.

Anyway, there we were, completely in awe of our unborn child, what with his/her crossed ankles and thumb-sucking prowess, when suddenly- the kid yawned.

Now, my husband has really big mouth. Not that he's loud (he's much more of a slow boil), but his wide mouth can open to unbelievably large proportions. Remember that Flip Top Head toothbrush campaign from the '80s and '90s? Even though the dude was a cartoon, it could have been P.J. His dentist once informed him that he has more than enough room for each wisdom tooth. This is both impressive, weird, and (I had thought) completely unique.

But now, here was this baby letting out a mammoth yawn from a downright unhinged jaw. P.J. actually welled up as he looked at me.

"That's my child!"

As pleased as I was to witness this act of father/child bonding, part of me was concerned that he had been unsure of parentage for a solid five months.

Shortly thereafter, we got a car.

This was a big milestone for us in terms of city dwelling. I could count on one hand the number of times that I've had to take a cab since I moved to Chicago; the transit system is that decent. A car just simply didn't even factor as a blip on our radar.

But then we realized that this future kid would need to be carted around, to places like the doctor's office and Taco Bell. And for about eight months out of the year, the weather here gets pretty nasty. I'd sloughed through the elements with many, many kiddos throughout the years, and it was rough enough to heft them (and their gear) into their parents' cars. I don't hate anyone enough to wish on them an early January morning bus ride with an infant. My Dad, who's had a dealership in his family for many years, had told us to let him know when we were ready for the whole car thing. In fact, the way we told my parents about our baby was by calling them up and suggesting that he start his search for a good used car in earnest.

My Dad had let out a quiet chuckle.

My Mom, confused, had demanded to know why we had put them both on speakerphone to talk about cars.

He soon found us a stellar VW Passat that I named The Grey Seal. Since the dealership was on the east coast, we had to arrange a time and place for a car transporter to deliver us our new car. This sounded pricey to us, but was surprisingly less costly than our original plan of buying two plane tickets back east, pulling an all-nighter to drive the vehicle back to Chicago, and most likely causing an accident on I-90 while falling asleep at the wheel. (Bail is expensive.)

The driver of the transporter called me multiple times on the drive to make sure that I was actually going to show up and retrieve the car. I assured him that I was, even though I was slightly concerned about his timeline. He was due to arrive anytime between 8am and 6pm- depending on traffic- and was adamant that we meet in a large, public lot. (For witnesses, I sagely acknowledged. My father patiently informed me that they needed room to park the car transporter. The Feds were most likely not going to be involved in this one.)

Even though it was a work day, I was able to finagle a fifteen minute block of time to run/waddle over to the closest grocery store, meet up with the trucker, and get the car. He was easy enough to spot. By this point in the pregnancy, so was I.

He was gruff and most likely exhausted. I had to pee and was craving something with red meat. But, since we weren't exactly destined to become pen pals, I forgave his attitude and he ignored my copious amount of sweat from the jaunt. (I really did run.)

He handed me the dealer plates and offered to put them on the car for me. Sure, I said. He held out his hand and asked if I had brought a screwdriver. (In the pocket of my jorts?) My admission that I did not, in fact, have a flathead screwdriver currently on my person seemed to solidify his opinion that I was utterly useless.

I didn't let that bother me. This car was totally mine, and I'd happily secure the license plate by tightening the screws with my thumbnail if I had to. (And I had to.)

I've dealt with lesser opinions of myself for way smaller payoffs.

The guy with all of the cars stacked haphazardly on his transporter took off for points west. I hopped into my lovely new sedan and had a momentary thought that I had totally duped The Man. There was no way in heck that I was responsible enough for all of this, but here I was. In my Big Kid car.

During the whole drive home that night, I kept waiting to be pulled over by The Reality Police. (Didn't happen. Probably because they don't exist. Still waited for them.)

P.J., ever the budgeter, had had concerns about this new expense. I somehow convinced him that it would actually *save* us money, even though I had no idea what I was talking about.

Anyhow, I like to think that P.J. was finally cool with the idea of the car because the love of his life, the mother of his unborn babe, was a cool person who deserved a Volkswagen and smooth transportation. This is probably not the case.

I highly suspect that, in his mind, the car already belonged to Schoeny Junior- or Juniorette- because the baby already ranked higher than anything he's known or touched or loved and who deserved to have the best of everything starting *now*.

I cared not. I still got a car.

CHAPTER FOUR

(Home Sweet...Good God, what's that smell?)

Since we were most likely going to be a family of three within a frighteningly short amount of time, we needed to make Big Decisions. Cram ourselves into our (nice) apartment and continue to pay rent, or spread out in a (possibly gross) home and go into crazy debt. Even with the potential to *eventually* save money, I kind of wonder what the heck we were thinking. But we had sipped the It's A Good Time To Buy Kool-Aid and there was no turning back. We were *going* to move into a house.

There was a home that we had toured the previous year with our first realtor, way back when house-hunting was still a whimsical game and not a depressing waltz through Scaryville. (We had long before come to grips with the fact that realtors and clients lost the desire to "stage" or "clean" homes when the price tag fell below three hundred thousand. And we weren't even anywhere near that lofty range.)

The house was on Troy Street and straddled the two emerging neighborhoods of Irving and Albany Park. It was on the higher spectrum of Places We Cannot Afford To Own But Which Sure Look Nice-ish and it was easily the biggest property we'd seen yet. It had three full floors of living space, front and back yards, a two car garage, a shed, and an eye-poppingly extravagant *two* kitchens. Sure, it had been a three-flat at some point in its past (and more recently a two-flat and, due to the tanking economy, had the distinct possibility of becoming a no-flat) but we viewed a second kitchen as the height of opulence and not a low-ceilinged basement convenience. On the tour that room was called the Summer Kitchen. Oh, and how I clung to that one. ("Darling, *a summer kitchen!*")

If you'll recall, we had very recently trudged through feces on linoleum.

The façade was a little strange, and stylistically the place couldn't decide if it was a wide brick bungalow with a vinyl-sided floor tacked on top, or if it was a rustily trimmed barn with a brick foundation. We were informed that it was built in 1959, but whether that date corresponded to the top floor addition or the chain link fence out front was anyone's guess. Regardless, I loved it instantly. P.J. thought it was okay, but that it really needed some work.

This was code for "Don't set your heart on it, we *cannot* afford it." Because if we were going to start bandying about the Needs Some Work disclaimer, well, this home would not even have cracked the top twelve.

The tour was a little strange, however, as we were guided in each room by the homeowner and her two small, sad-faced kiddos. The woman's husband had recently passed away from a sudden illness and the woman had really wanted to sell us on the place. This made us feel even more rotten about casually viewing a property out of our price range (something we mentally swore on the spot to never ever do again, ever). Each time we commented on how much we liked a feature, the woman informed us that her husband had worked really hard on that. And reminded us that he had died. And then asked if we wanted to make an offer. It was more than a little awkward.

Even with the currently large asking price, they had recently gone into foreclosure and needed to sell the place, fast. Her husband had been the one in the process of converting the home back into a single family residence and he had added such great features as sporadic flooring and drywall. It made us realize how rough this place must've been if, years into a renovation project, there was still a ridiculous amount of work left to do.

But, although I immediately felt drawn to this odd house, I had to side with P.J. and admit that we really couldn't swing that kind of money. It went off the market soon thereafter and we assumed that the bank had taken ownership.

We [I] put it on our [my] Nothing Will Compare To That House list and carried on looking at tiny homes with soggy carpeting and death-defying staircases.

But then, a short while later, The Troy House came back on the market as a short sale. For one hundred and fifty thousand less.

On one hand, we felt really badly for the poor lady and her kids who had lost their home. Awful, even. On the other hand, we suddenly had the opportunity to buy a great house for a ridiculously cheap price. The second thought made us feel like terrible people. We still wanted to grab the place for ourselves, but we readily admitted that we were horrid.

P.J. saw the listing within minutes of its posting. Disregarding the comments of "foreclosure" and "needs work," we made an appointment to see the place again- with our new (awesome) realtor. We were the first ones to see it this time around.

In the relatively short time since we had last viewed it, the house had lain empty and was stripped of all appliances, baseboards, light fixtures and a garage door. The dining room, which had been the children's bedroom, had a ceiling covered with stickers and Crayola markings. We snarkily asked ourselves, "Bounce on the bed, much?" Even thinking that thought made me feel instantly and horrifically bad. You just lost your home and your father, children. Draw on the ceiling if you want to. Heck, draw on my face.

The lower level bedroom was completely empty except for one gigantic cockroach which, upon Googling its image, I found was only indigenous to Texas. Before I could even utter it, P.J. shot down my suggestion that the cockroach was haunting us. Because, apparently, Texan ghost bugs do not exist.

The first floor picture window at the back of the house had been shattered, and there was evidence of people and/or rodents taking up temporary residence.

Attached to the garage was a shed that was a huge mess of rat feces, smushed ketchup packets (and/or blood), and a heavy odor that permeated every corner. This was not a selling point to me, although the extra storage apparently made the property go up P.J.'s estimation. Boys are weird.

We found out from neighbors that the family who owned the place prior to this family had a slightly bizarre past. Teenagers with drug habits and criminal records were the reason the third floor window had been shot out and covered with pink foam core until a replacement window could be found. (Of which a replacement was apparently hard to find, since it was still bright pink ten years later.) Also, all of the bedroom doors possessed locks *on the outsides*. Mommie Dearest-tacular! A closet in the lower level bedroom featured an interior door leading directly outside, right under the concrete front stoop. This cold and dark hidey hole had a glass block window on one wall and no other means of light or escape. The same neighbor told us that this was a room where the teenagers would go during police raids. I chose to imagine it as a bit of a speakeasy. That seemed a little more "flapper era" and a little less "where we hid the bodies".

There was also an elaborate L-shaped closet under the basement stairs that I immediately dubbed The Harry Potter Closet, since it seemed like someone could live there (or be forced to live there) quite comfortably, insofar as closet-living goes. The creepiest part of the closet (besides the whole "living under the stairs" bit) was a tossup between the miniature shelves at the far end of the L-shape which featured one and a half foot high ceilings, and the spiky nails sticking out of the interior doorframe. All numbered.

The living room had long, deep grooves dug into the hardwood floors where appliances had been dragged out. There was a strange smell coming from the basement. The third floor bathroom had been covered with red winterizing powder that, when smudged, looked like a crime scene. And the master bedroom featured scrawled graffiti so intense that it would make a sailor cringe.

But it still had a lot of things going for it. It was simply the biggest place we had seen within city limits (within our price range). The neighborhood boasted good trains and buses and some of the best food in Chicago. Lebanese bakeries, tamale stands, and frighteningly cheap produce; a delicious triumvirate. It had multiple picture windows, both at the front and rear of the house, and the brick was sturdy. In fact, it was easily the hardiest structure and had the most working windows and doors of any property we had seen. All of that space just seemed to beg for creativity to be unleashed.

And there was more than enough room for a strawberry patch in the garden, too.

The home definitely felt sad to me, though. I couldn't help but feel like it was waiting for us to come make it happy again. It could've just as easily been the hormones careening through me and demanding that I anthropomorphize everything. (Girls can be weird, too.)

Even with all of the freakish things going on in this home, it was obvious that it could be made into a pretty cool place.

We made an offer.

I felt so good about this place that I snuck over in the middle of the day to plant a peony bush in the desolate, abandoned lot of a backyard. This was a full month before our offer was accepted.

And sure, the plant was a freebie from the Arbor Day Foundation and the only other option I had was to let the thing die in the apartment fridge, which seemed wrong. So I drove to the house one afternoon and crept around back to give the home a pretty little gift (which wouldn't blossom for another three years).

During the process of buying this home I continued to believe that the property was haunted, even beyond the cockroach. Not Scooby Doo haunted (as my childlike sensibilities refuse to let me view anything that mainstream America would deem a true horror movie) but a definite presence could be felt.

Turns out, an exorcism would've been way cheaper. Within moments of arriving at the house, our home inspector informed us that we needed a new tear-off roof, boiler, and water heater, and had to somehow convert the ancient electrical system back to a single family residence, as opposed to the three-flat it had been in the process of becoming.

But look how much space! That was the refrain that P.J. and I would chant to each other. Like a mantra. Or the kind of thing that people mutter to themselves as they rock in the corner at the mental institution.

My first indication of Money-Pitness should've been apparent after the inspector's initial reactions. Having turned on the kitchen tap to see about pressure and drainage, he decided to let it run for a bit while he checked on the exterior brick. Lagging behind as everyone walked to the side of the house, I couldn't help but feel that something was slightly amiss. I heard a *whoosh* and chalked it up to traffic or wind. When it didn't abate, I poked my head back into the house and heard a rumbling and gurgling that brought to mind only one explanation.

Ghosts.

As it grew louder, I stepped into the house and peeked into the kitchen to see water. Tons of it. I am only slightly ashamed to admit that I screamed. My husband bolted back into the house and was followed by the realtor and inspector.

I choose to believe that P.J.'s rapid fire response was due to the fact that he believed I was being attacked by ghosts, but he (outwardly) denies this.

Water was pouring over the sides of the double sink and, as we soon discovered, was spurting out of the pipes in the cabinet. Okay, we agreed, so the sink was clogged. Problem solved as soon as we turned off the tap and drained the sink, right? Except for the fact that water was still spilling out onto the floor and we were currently inside a stripped, abandoned and empty house. We had nothing with which to empty the sink.

Always quick with questionable split-second decisions, I shoved my finger into the burst pipe. (To be fair, I was exhausted by this point. Ghosts, water, barely staved-off morning sickness? I was fine with sitting down, even if it meant losing circulation in my hand.)

So now we had a full sink, a pregnant woman in very real danger of losing a digit, water everywhere, and still no vessel in sight.

The inspector went out to his truck.

P.J. spoke vaguely about buying some sort of bucket-like thing and drove off to find the nearest store. Keeping in mind that we did not know this neighborhood and the proximity of useful stores that sold bucket-like objects, I despaired of ever seeing him again. (Or my finger.)

People took turns attempting to dump the sink water into the non-working toilet; a ripped plastic grocery bag was used, an empty travel coffee mug, and my cupped hand once I regained feeling (and had someone else plug the hole with *their* finger.)

This was an intensely hands-on (fingers-on?) experience to be having in a house that wasn't even mine.

As we were nearing the end of the deluge, P.J. arrived bearing two flower pots. They were lovely flower pots, but unfortunately each one possessed a rather big drainage hole in the bottom.

There is a distinct point in the home-buying/pregnancy process where all involved parties' heads explode. P.J. had passed that point about a mile back, right around the time that the pregnancy became very real and we suddenly had to figure out where in Chicago we'd be placing the kid's bedroom. (He returned the flower pots for store credit.)

The good news was that the sink was not beyond all hope. And the only areas that got soaked were the stained countertops and the cracked ceramic tile floor, both of which needed to be replaced anyhow. Score one for selective flooding!

Shortly after the inspection (which yielded an alarmingly thick volume of checklist warnings) but well before we actually bought the house, I went ahead and placed an order to repair the lower level's shattered picture window. P.J. was not pleased with me about this one and wished I would stop trespassing to fix up someone else's home. His logic was that we should actually "own" a place before "making changes." My point of view was that any manner of critter- or worse- was able to come and go willy-nilly. I really wanted to kibosh that. Besides, who knew how long a work order like that could take? I was certain that some guy at the glass place would call me back within a month or two and we'd be legitimate homeowners by then.

Turns out, it took two days. The window and glass shop was half a block away from the house and they were more than happy to walk over and measure, stroll back to the store, return with the necessary parts, and build us a sparkling new window in a matter of hours. And since it didn't cost an arm and a leg, I was able to convince P.J. that, even with the worst case scenario of the house deal falling through, we had done something nice for the house. Even if we were technically breaking and entering, it was for the greater good. That's right, I had technically broken into a home that belonged to a bank and repaired part of it.

P.J. thought I had fully lost my marbles. He also begged me not to tell anyone about it. I assured him that I wouldn't.

We went full steam ahead with purchasing the Troy house in July, keeping in the back of our minds the laundry list of things needing immediate attention, at least according to the inspector. (Looking back, we probably didn't give his warnings enough weight, as things like "faulty wiring" and "dangerous water heater" were listed alongside "crack in the sidewalk- too many weeds.")

We put in our offer, beating out a few other interested

parties because we didn't have a home to sell on contingency. To tell the truth, the home-buying process didn't seem very real at all. We half expected a hidden camera to reveal itself at any second and deem us too young and stupid to own a home.

Turns out, we were just young and stupid enough.

All involved parties found us competent enough to sign away the next thirty years and our life savings. Which rather disproves the idea of competency, I think.

The closing was a very serious and lengthy affair consisting of- as best I can remember- signing thousands of papers and riders and contracts, and trying to keep from nervously giggling like a moron. I signed so many things that my signature on those forms was completely unrecognizable. I managed to drop all consonants, leaving a big flouncy 'K' and a string of orphaned vowels. Apparently it was still legit.

As we were handed the keys, our (awesome) realtor drolly told us, "Congratulations. You just bought a big, ugly house."

Nothing could have dampened our spirits. This large and rambling house was ours. We were thrilled by the prospect of sitting on a real estate goldmine. (Or rickety money and time-suck. Who really has a crystal ball for these things?) We owned it and no one in the whole world- to the best of our immediate knowledge- could say otherwise.

Unfortunately, that meant that we'd actually have to *live* there.

Despite having spent enough time on the closing that we could have built an actual house, that didn't could towards "time served." We still had a mortgage that threatened to outlast our marriage. And, excepting an illegally replaced brand new window in a broken kitchen and a wilting peony bush in the yard, we had to start from scratch on fixing up a good majority of the house.

It had been a dream of mine that, once we were homeowners, P.J. could heft me across a threshold. Sadly, in order for this to become a reality, one has to possess a working threshold. I was also approaching Way Too Big To Heft status.

Threshold aside, we had a whole lot of buying to do. Our list of things to find/replace included: (other) windows, doors, baseboards, door frames, ceiling fans, a roof, a boiler, a water heater, and a garage door. Plus all of the appliances that are generally seen inside of a home. This was our starting-off point.

The boiler itself could have been an apt metaphor for our new home. It looked weird; a gargantuan, ugly, and bizarre structure with copper pipes sticking out every which way; seeming for all the world like a really sloppy time machine. And it was *so old* that every single plumber who came to quote estimates for the thing exclaimed that they had never before seen anything so ancient. None of them even knew what kind it was. Just that it didn't work and would take a miracle (and a pack of Clydesdales) to remove from the premises. Because it was broken. Very, very broken.

The plumber we eventually picked dissected the machine into about eight ridiculously heavy pieces, making some neighborhood scrapper light up like Christmas morning. (We had previously been uninformed about the art form of scrap metal snatching: Hordes of flatbed trucks slyly cruising alleys, looking for the faintest gleam of metal to throw into the back. Sometimes we would leave small things on the trashcan lids, like a strange little offering. I like to think that it worked. One time we left a massive window treatment that was reminiscent of an office park's blinds, circa 1970. It was a honking strip of metal rods and forest green plastic blinds that went all the way to the floor. Within an hour of placing it outside, all that was left of it was a stack of plastic; almost like a metal-eating monster had spit the plastic bones back out.)

A sane person would have panicked at the time/money/expertise it would require to make our dream of living indoors a reality. Although, a sane person probably wouldn't have undertaken a feat this laughable so close to birthing an actual human being, so perhaps my parameters for sanity need tweaking. However, I had the safety net known as: My Parents.

My Dad had been a carpenter and handyman for a number of years when I was a kid. I saw him put up a garage and sunroom largely by himself. Surely this house was akin to a garage/sunroom combo, right? He wouldn't even need to deal with that pesky foundation thing! And if there's a mess my Mom can't handle, I haven't yet seen it- nor would I like to.

They showed up the week after we bought the place and a couple of weeks before we had the big move-in. I imagine they had expected they'd do a little patching, a little scrubbing, and take us out for some deep dish. What ended up happening was the car got loaded up every morning at 7am, proving that automobiles are useful things not just for the carting around of babies. We each brought two sets of clothing; stuff to wear for a solid thirteen hours of manual labor, and the items we changed into while we buried or burned the former.

The first day they saw the new place was also the day a crew arrived to do a full tear-off roof. A team of guys showed up early, stayed late, and *tore off that roof.* Maybe two guys in the whole bunch spoke English. I didn't mind, because they didn't want to speak to me, anyhow. Throughout the day, multiple layers of roofing were flung with lightning speed into the general direction of the dumpster parked on our curb.

A generally acknowledged rule (of which I had also been blissfully ignorant) is that no more than three layers of roof patching can occur before it just gets ridiculous. Our roof possessed at least seven. It was like a strange kindergarten pasting project.

When they removed all of the layers, they were surprised

to find a hole that poked right into the master bedroom closet. (I was not surprised.) Then, with equal lightning speed, they fixed the roof and slapped some new tar up there.

There were a few casualties, however, from the constantly falling roof shingles. One was a rosebush in the front yard. The second was our next door neighbor's side door light (and his budding goodwill).

The first was easily amended with a little trimming and know-how from my mother. The second never really got definitive closure, other than copious apologies and offers to replace the thing.

Few things linger like the hairy eyeball of an elderly Filipino neighbor.

July in Chicago can be brutal. This summer was no exception, and the only way we got air into the house was when my Dad installed ceiling fans that turned and kind of moved the musty air around. The only fan on the third floor needed to be removed because a) it was broken and b), with a ceiling height of 8ft and blades that reached down to 6ft (at an angle!), we were relegating any visitors to a positively *Highlander* fate. We called it the Fan of Death and laughed hysterically.

Most likely this was due to a very real lack of air.

My father patched so much drywall that I'm pretty sure that, by this point, the walls are largely created by him. He built magical things such as doorways and solidified concepts such as "corners of a room."

My Mom cleaned the inaccurately named "master" bathroom and I was able to enter that room for the first time. (Aversion to certain rooms was most likely an issue that should've been dealt with pre-closing. Live and learn.)

She also managed to remove a huge pile of hardened glop from the countertops. Let's go ahead and say it was some sort of home repair material. Maybe some type of animal byproduct home repair material. She also thoroughly removed any traces of unmentionable stuff from the cabinets which, if we *must* mention them, included a fully petrified onion. (I felt for the onion. I was petrified, too.)

Conservatively, we averaged nine trips to The Home Depot each day. With the amount of stuff we purchased, we qualified for a pretty sweet Home Depot card. Heck, with the amount of stuff we purchased, we most likely put someone at The Home Depot through college. And that whole cliché about homeowners spending their weekends there? Totally true, because the ridiculous amount of stuff that needs to be done with even a semi-working house requires parts and tools you won't realize you require until you return home from your latest Home Depot trip.

Sadly, my parents had to return home to the East coast later that week. My Mom later informed me that my Dad, usually the bastion of stoicism, actually teared up as they boarded the plane, admitting his guilt at leaving me in a house that ramshackle. I chose to believe that the emotions were stemming from a complete lack of sleep and hydration, rather than the very real possibility that my father believed me to be residing in a papier-maché house.

My mother demanded that we take it easy, telling us that Rome wasn't built in a day. Although, as she admitted, Troy was certainly being rehabbed on a tight deadline.

We now had less than a week until The Big Move In and a ton of work to do, especially on that whole "interior" thing. We had recently come to terms with the fact that, exterior-wise, we'd be the neighborhood Boo Radley house for the next handful of years.

Between the time that we had last seen the house and now, the kitchen's window turns had disappeared. Up until this point, it had never occurred to me that these things existed independently of the actual windows. But they were gone. The kitchen had a big picture window with two vertical screened windows that opened out to the sides; that is, when the mechanism to do so was still in place. At the base of these windows was a gaping hole apiece. Now, what someone thought they could do with these little knobs out in the world is anyone's guess, but I'll tell you what we did. Nothing. No one, not even the window's manufacturer, not Home Depot, *not even the internet* could tell us how to replace the things independently of buying a whole new picture window. (And I'd already checked off one of those purchases from my bucket list.)

Since the lack of turns fell under the newly created Annoying Yet Not Glaringly Crucial category of fixing up our home, we started opening the windows by raising the screen and shoving the glass partition outwards. Closing them required pulling the frame towards oneself and quickly pushing down on the screen lock to drag it a little closer. (Or, as I liked to refer to it: Asking P.J. To Do It For Me.)

Appliances were easy enough, at least initially. We chose a dishwasher, stove, washer and dryer. Friends of ours who were renovating their own kitchen had generously given us their stainless steel fridge for a scant fraction of the cost, so we at least had a way to store some food. (Even if we could no longer afford it.)

We measured (and re-measured) the dimensions for each appliance, setting up a day for appliance delivery a tad close to the day that we'd be moving in. The washer and dryer were installed with no problems. And man, for longtime apartment dwellers, this was a thing worth celebrating. Free laundry! (Except for the water and electricity and detergent.)

Then it came time for the dishwasher to be installed. This was another big deal purchase. In my mind, it equated never having to "do" the dishes ever again. (Because rinsing, loading, drying, and putting dishes away didn't equate to "doing" them.)

And the thing fit in its space just fine, as long as one never needed to close the door to actually turn the dishwasher on. Our hideous countertop had foiled us again, this time with an improbably long overhang. And we couldn't afford to replace the much-reviled counter, *because we had just purchased a dishwasher.* So the appliance had to go back to the store and we had to figure out what the next "standard" size down was. And as soon as possible too, since there was a gaping hole under the counter which caused security concerns for me. Basically, I wanted to seal up any access points for rodents, creepy crawlies, and ghosts.

Next, in came the stove. I had never even seen a brand new stove, aside from on HGTV. And it was gorgeous. (It looked like it did all of those important cooking functions as well.) It was a good thing I liked the look of it, because it stood in the center of my kitchen for a few hours. The countertop that abutted where the new stove was to live was- and I quote one of the delivery guys- "an irregular length" and it didn't allow for the stove to slide into place. (That damn countertop again!) So he was going to take it back to the store.

The room became stiflingly hot. I couldn't quite wrap my head around the idea that I needed to make an immediate decision which would affect the very real possibility of working appliances *not* residing in our house for the next few weeks. I couldn't decide what would be worse: having gaping appliance holes in the kitchen/no method of cooking food/potential gateways into rodent hell while we actually resided there? Or viewing the stove in the center of the room (and not in an artful "island" way) and a dishwasher hanging open on a daily basis? Even though this decision wasn't as important as, say, debating whether or not the baby's room needed ventilation (yes), or how long we could go without an actual garage door (a month and a half), I couldn't make this call. So, I'll admit it, I cried. A lot. Call it the Pregnancy Card, or the Overwhelmed Female Homeowner, or any other repulsive excuse for but it made the deliverymen extraordinarily uncomfortable.

"Do you want us to put this one back on the truck, too?"

No, I did *not*. I wanted something as benign as countertops to work the way they were supposed to, the way they did on television and in books and in glossy magazines, the ones where bowls of fruit never had fruit flies and food in the crisper never rotted into goop. I didn't expect or need high-end fixtures, but I also didn't expect to be done in by chipped Formica. What I wanted was a kitchen where stoves did not live diagonally to the fridge, and ones where dishwasher-sized holes in the stupidly sized counters did not smell strongly of mouse pee and despair. I accepted that this home's floors would have holes, and I was tolerating a general lack of functioning windows, but every person has her limits.

I babbled something to this effect in the direction of the remaining deliveryman (his associate had long before excused himself to the relative sanity of the outdoors) and continued to

Ugly Cry at him.

Tentatively, he asked me again if I wanted to keep it or have them take it. Free of charge, like that should shift my mood.

I began my spiel again, backed up by a fresh set of tears, but was quickly cut off.

"Look, do you care about this counter?"

"No, I *hate* it-"

And, like that, he scraped the side of the counter with a box cutter and proceeded to slam the stove into its (forever and ever) home.

He received a generous tip.

Here's a fun way to find out who your true friends are: A) Get pregnant. B) Buy a dilapidated house. C) Wait by the door. (But only if your home possesses one.)

Our real pals repeatedly showed up wearing paint-splattered overalls, clutching a bag of tacos and inquiring as to what needed patchin'. Sure, we had slight suspicions that one or two of them may have been high as kites during their forays into helpfulness. (How else to explain multiple cans of paint being knocked over and emptied, and "completed" rooms with virtually no paint in danger of touching the tops of the walls? Some of the walls looked like big ol' Rothko paintings. Lots of square sections of smashed color with a conservative amount of border.) But we also had friends who made short work of bedrooms and stairwells and helped to salvage hideous fixtures. And they didn't even question our color choices. This is clutch. Because- and we all know this- people naturally judge garish palettes in magazines and during open houses. But as soon as you choose Cajun Red in the living room, a good friend needs to agree that you've made the perfect choice. And then paint that living room Cajun Red.

We had other acquaintances who cheerfully informed that they'd be by for dinner some evening to play with the baby. *Not if there's no floor on which to place a table, you won't,* was the muttered retort under my New Englandesque polite smile. It had never occurred to us that our friend base was so sharply divided; long past were the days where friends could be bribed to help move apartments with only beer and pizza as compensation. We understood that. Because that type of friendship request definitely has a shelf life. And once you've whittled down the friends-of-friends and the casual acquaintances of your post-college youth, you're left with (if you're extremely lucky) a group of pals who don't (outwardly) mind doing exhausting work on a place in which they don't even reside, just because they like you as person and want your life to be nice.

We considered ourselves extremely lucky.

That's not to say that the renovations just zipped along

smoothly from there. P.J. and I possessed different work styles, and that occasionally slowed down the progress. P.J. was (and is) of the cautious camp. The thrifty camp. The Let's See What The Internet/Experts/Our Folks Say About Rewiring This Ourselves camp.

We almost got divorced the day that I discovered P.J. attempting to remove pieces of blue painter's tape from itself (although he might disagree and believe that our imminent demise almost occurred eleven instances prior). He tried to convince me that we would be saving buckets of money, what with the crazy amounts of rooms and baseboards left to paint-tape. I argued that a roll of paint tape cost a couple of bucks, and that he had already wasted more time in the unraveling than it would've taken to walk to Home Depot and back. *And time is money.* That was my new catchphrase. The kind that's yelled on a street corner by an insane person. *You're going to hell! Have you met my cat?! Time is money! The sky is potatoes!*

It's a slippery slope from being an ignorant first-time homeowner to being a lunatic ranting on the curb.

As for me, I'm of the Get It Done variety. Make-It-Work Flynn is what P.J. once termed me, and it wasn't the most loving of monikers.

I found myself securing things with whatever was handy. (Because nothing stays put like things fastened with that special blend of found objects, ineptitude, and a nice dash of impatience.)

Once I got going, nothing would slow down the trajectory of my project. Everything within arm's reach would become a tool, a thing to stand on, or a clever means to hide ugly parts of the house. When a curtain rod was too short to reach across the family room picture window's length, I inserted a random pole into one half of the rod to act as an extender. I thought that this was a brilliant idea for three reasons: We *had* the pole right there, Home Depot was closed for the evening, and P.J. would be proud of my penny-pinching ways. (He wasn't. Turns out, he preferred "actual hardware.")

P.J. would attempt to reason with me, telling me that perhaps a screw shouldn't be used as a drill bit, standing on a swiveling stool while hammering wasn't wise, and that my drop cloth was his favorite hoodie. I took his advice with a grain of salt.

Some people just fear progress.

Early in the process I tried to be as careful as humanly possible. For the baby, of course. Paint fumes! Heavy lifting! Non-elevated ankles! That was the trifecta of pregnancy warnings, and I heeded them. Initially.

Except for one ill-advised occasion when I tripped off of a step stool while attempting to hang lights in the downstairs family room. Sure, it could have waited until P.J. joined me that evening, but something about being in that empty cave-like room screamed "Hang up Christmas lights around the perimeter of the room on your day off!" to me. (And I listened.)

The baby was totally fine, most likely because I landed on my elbow. I promised the baby that I'd be nicer/more careful/less of an unfit mother from this point out, but I think we both knew who the raging liar was.

It just wasn't possible to *not* keep going full steam. Every time I thought about the rapidly approaching time bomb that was our due date, I needed to sand, heft, and paint, pausing every few moments to stick my head out the window and breathe real air. (Near a major bus route and our chain-smoking neighbors.) And what made me throw caution to the smoggy wind was the realization that the child I was carrying was going to have to live here, too, for its *first home*. Where it had to lie down and breathe and eventually put things into its mouth.

The baby's bedroom, a vibrant mash up of teal and maroon walls, was beyond depressing, even with the bonus of its soundproofed ceiling. The paint I had chosen for the baby's room was a pastel- Pale Sunshine- a choice I later rued because of its utter inability to hide the walls' previous lives. Another reason for regret: I was later informed that yellow on a wall made babies angry. Yellow! Even if it's termed something as innocuous as "sunshine." Go figure. But do you know what else makes babies angry? Nurseries that could moonlight as death carnivals.

After working on the house for one long stretch the week before we moved in, I had my second breakdown as a homeowner. This was the big freaked-out temper tantrum, the one that began this tale.

P.J. had recently left for a performance and my friends had put down the paintbrushes to go act, drink, dance, and live as actual human beings. (They had my blessing/envy.) So what happened after I cried at ugly walls and lamented a frightening amount of my life choices?

I went and got a taco, extra onions. (Oh, who am I kidding? Extra everything.)

And then I came back to the house and gave myself a pep talk.

You're good at cleaning and fixing, I told myself.

This is totally something you wanted so do your damn job, I told myself.

Your problems are not valid; people are dying from awful diseases and our American judicial system is horribly flawed, I told myself. (I never claimed to be motivational.)

Feeling sufficiently guilty and more than a little full, I tackled the kitchen floor. (How's that for a visual? A beached whale belly-flopping onto an ocean of hideous ceramic tile.)

Not surprisingly, I hadn't been able to find an exact match for the Kelly green swirled flooring, so I made do with a matte green tile that matched it not at all. I wasn't thrilled with spending the money for something that would still appear to be more than a little slapdash, but I didn't have much of a choice. The new tile needed to cover holes that went straight down to the lower level. It was like an ugly sea of poorly placed wishing wells.

I could have used one right about then. For instance, I wished my floor wasn't made of Swiss cheese. (Also that we were still renters, but there's no sense in living with the Woulda Couldas, now is there?)

Scraping the grout and cement for the handful of tiles that needed replacing seemed like it should only take a little while. After all, we were talking about a few twelve inch squares, here. Spread out over two full rooms and a hallway.

It made me contemplate just why the ugliest flooring choices seemed to cover the greatest area in the home. Newton must have had a law for that. Or one of his friends did. Maybe one of the poor, artistic ones.

It took me nearly three days to fix that unattractive floor. But after I was finished with the scraping and patching and grouting, the kitchen floor was a borderline tidy checkerboard of neatly placed (though mismatched) tiles. And since the floors now cleanly met the bottoms of the walls, I was so pleased that I wouldn't have minded if the tiles were neon yellow and puce. The idea that something in the home looked roughly how something would look in a "normal" home did a lot for my state of mind.

However, since I was certain that *someone* of a vaguely haunting nature was looking over my shoulder whenever I was alone in any room, perhaps my state of mind shouldn't have been used as any sort of yardstick.

While we were dipping our toes into the ocean of home repair, I was still working full time and carrying the kickiest child known to [wo]man. And while the first trimester Awfuls had mercifully ended, the exhaustion had not yet let up. I suspected that this second trimester- the Feeling Good one- was still plagued with daily drowsiness because of the ineptitude with which we were playing Bob Vila. I was extraordinarily cross at the knowledge that I was squandering the only part of this pregnancy where I was supposed to feel awesome.

I knew that I had lost the ability for rational thought while at work one day with one of my toddlers. We were playing with her babies and dollhouse, and I began to envy the perfection of her three story plastic Fisher-Price home. Just seeing all of those molded little heads enjoying furniture and countertops made me tear up with unrestrained jealousy and despair. My house would *never* have clean lines like that! Nor would it have as clean of floors. *Their* baby got to have a finished nursery. I bet their windows and doors even opened and latched.

Jerks.

CHAPTER FIVE

(Well, THAT was foolhardy!)

So, we moved in.

"What?" you seem to ask. "That place hardly seemed people-ready."

Correct. It was not. We still had lumber and tools shoved into corners where projects still desperately needed to be completed. There would be time to finish things like baseboards, we told ourselves. Having furniture and boxes in front of these areas shouldn't impede us too much.

We had previously decided to clear what usable floor space we had to make room for the smallish amount of apartment-filling things we owned. After all, it was an apartment. How hard could it be to fit everything into a home roughly three times its size?

Turns out, we are guppies. You know how they grow to fit the size of their fishbowls? We were so good at being guppies that our possessions expanded upon leaving our tidy apartment, causing our new rooms to look like an episode of Hoarders. I'm pretty sure that people stopped to buy things along the mile-long stretch to our new place. There's really no other explanation.

One of my best friends possessed extraordinary British

sensibilities and had packed most of our apartment within an inch of its life. But regardless of how well she and I had labeled things, I forgot to take into account that our eight over-caffeinated movers spoke not a word of English. So, the "nursery" became the foyer. "Keely's craft projects" were upended into the appliance-free second kitchen. Just as well. That was an obnoxious label for a moving box.

For a short while, P.J. had stationed me at the side door to our new home where I was supposed to help guide the movers to various rooms in the house. Now, my high school Spanish was so-so, unless I was feeling self-conscious about it. (And I was feeling self-conscious about it.)

After a few minutes of failing to properly field questions and direct them (because for some reason, the only room name I could recall was "baño"), the movers started to blatantly ignore me as they whipped boxes up and down the stairs. I was convinced that they were laughing at me.

Before the situation imploded into a supernova of extreme heat, temper, and hypersensitivity, P.J. assigned me the quite crucial task of checking on the potted plants.

Our cats were having an ever rougher time of it than I was. P.J. and I were the proud, over-attentive owners to a tabby and his fluffy little brother. Ender and Bean. They were our pre-baby babies, and they really got the short end of the moving stick.

I had been so concerned that they'd be able to run outside (and away forever!) during Moving Day that I had confined them to two separate cat carriers and placed them in the empty bathroom for safety. This seemed to suit everyone just fine until one of our multitude of moving guys used the bathroom. He splattered water (I hope) onto the carriers in the absence of any towels or shower curtain on which to dry his hands. The bathroom was used twice in this manner at the apartment, and then once more at the new house. Besides being a slob, I also suspected that he had an unchecked urinary tract infection.

So the damp and trapped pets started the day in a dark and bizarre place, only to get moved into the now-empty second bedroom of the old apartment while we drove ourselves and the remaining houseplants over to the new abode. Our reasoning had been that we could leave them at the old place for an hour or two and they could enjoy the familiar look and smell of their old hangout. (Outside of their crates, obviously. We're not *monsters!*) We'd save them the stress of the doors opening and closing a trillion times and strangers galore tramping around and potentially peeing on them.

Except, we forgot to take into account how incredibly creepy it might be for them to be left in a room they loved, sans furniture. Especially knowing for a fact that everything they knew was missing on the other side of the bedroom door. Including their previously kind owners.

We returned an hour (or three) later to find one feral cat

and his terrified little brother. They were both wedged behind the room's skinny radiator, although one had spikes for fur and the other had eyes entirely comprised of pupil. They wanted nothing to do with us or each other, and even less to do with the carriers into which they suspected they were to be shoved.

The backseat of the Passat's new soundtrack was a low keening so incredibly mournful that it made me regret all of my life choices. It was the saddest place on Earth.

Coming in a close second was the new house's lower level.

We had figured that it would be best to let them out into the basement laundry room where their litter boxes would now reside. But what a terrible first image of a home! Ender skulked around the perimeter of the room, eventually scoping the downstairs and darting up to the bedrooms like his tail was afire. Bean refused to exit his carrier for a good ten hours.

It took a few weeks before they'd remain in a room which we had entered. Longer still for eye contact to be reestablished. Towards the end of the summer they allowed us to pet them once more.

"Phewf," they said to us (in voices that only cat owners give to their overindulged pets), "Glad things are back to normal."

I didn't have the heart to tell them what the Fall would bring.

The cats weren't the only ones airing grievances on moving day. My bed, the pot of gold at the end of Moving Day's dim little rainbow, refused to fit up the narrow stairs to the third floor. The mattress would fit, and all of the bedding with it, but not the bed frame nor anything else that would allow me to believe I wasn't camping. It was left in the stairwell for a few hours before being moved to its new home in the lower level's second kitchen, where it would live for a good three months. Thus, my inaugural act as a second trimester, first time homeowner, was to sleep on the floor of an attic bedroom without a working window.

I am told that the sound of someone crying themselves to sleep beside you is not the most peaceful of sounds.

We went to Ikea.

Again, here was the unmistakable envy associated with home perfection. I wanted to live in their bedroom level. Sure, there were entirely too many people milling about with plates of miniature Swedish meatballs, but that seemed like a really tiny price to pay for an insane amount of shelving. Besides, I could eat in their café every day. I practically closed them down that afternoon as it was, since our tray was laden with five plates of food. (Note to Ikea: bigger trays wouldn't be a bad investment.)

We found a bed with dark wood and a non-obnoxious headboard. (Here is an example of why a marriage can work. My husband understands what a "non-obnoxious headboard" means and why it is crucial against a wall with a window. Also, he is willing to pretend that the majority of the five plates on the tray are his.) This fabulous bed also had one pivotal feature: it broke apart into multiple convenient pieces, just perfect for hoisting up a skinny excuse for a staircase.

No sooner had we gotten our bed home (along with some really lovely curtains and a few other necessary purchases grabbed right by the checkout aisle) that P.J. had to leave again. His mother had taken the bus into town for the weekend and he needed to drive to the terminal and pick her up. He left really strict instructions for me to rest, since it was boiling hot and the kiddo inside of me was threatening to stage a coup of elbows and knees. I was *most certainly* not to touch the boxed-up bed.

And I tried. But I couldn't get comfy on the lower level couch knowing that, mere floors above, was the answer to my late-pregnancy sleeping needs. And this miracle was being contained in three cinchy boxes.

Perhaps the bed would even come in handy later than that; like maybe even once I had delivered the child and returned to normal sleeping positions. I held only the smallest amount of hope that that day would come, because pregnancy had made me remarkably fatalistic.

So I opened the boxes. No strain there. A box cutter did that job for me. And sure, the planks for the platform support were the tiniest bit heavy, but I made do with lifting them out individually. Except for the smallish ones near the end.

I laid out the pieces like the outline of a bed, forgoing the completely inane Ikea directions. I really had no choice, if you think about it. After opening the cartoony pamphlet and seeing that you would need the help of two balding men without discernible clothing, what would *you* have done?

Besides, it was really stressful to see that bald guy with a big x over his face every time he tried to do something; lift something by himself, use a different tool than his friend's l-shaped widget, hold a board up high... No wonder he was frowning.

I went full steam ahead with the building of this bed, quite confident in the knowledge that one pregnant American more than equaled two bald Scandinavians who hear nothing but "no" all day. My patriotic pride kept me going for a little while, but shortly thereafter I acknowledged how nice it would've been to have had one of those balding Nordic men hold the pieces level while I spun a teensy screw with a child-sized metal L.

I decided that I had had enough of this. Enough blazing heat, enough rib cracking from my child, enough of that *smell* (Good Lord, was our downstairs moonlighting as the town dump?) and certainly enough of the dinky equipment that wasn't getting the job done.

So I went against the cartoon directions yet again and got my power drill. (That action warranted *two* big ol' exes over it in the Ikea manual. That poor guy can't even take a breath without being exed out.) I also used some better screws. It was like swatting a fly with a cannonball. But those boards are *attached*.

And for the record, the instructions guesstimated that the bed assembly would take roughly five hours. I got it done in an hour and a half.

There's a good chance that this bed will never leave this house. But that's fine, because I decided on that day that I would die there, in that bed. In a far off time, obviously. I wasn't going to end it all before getting to enjoy the fruits of my labor.

Speaking of that, this was around when I actively started to fantasize about giving birth. Sure, there would be some mild unpleasantness but, from what I had heard, they had beds in the hospitals. Also, cable.

By the time P.J. and his mother returned, I was a humongous, achy, sweaty mess. With a bed that would never need fear a hurricane.

P.J., concerned, asked if he could help. Because, as everyone knows, the crucial time for help in a situation like this is during the last five minutes. However, he's a smart guy. He wisely didn't mention the questionable activity on my part, only how gorgeous the bed looked. And me. Especially me.

Two days later, men arrived to fix one broken window. Not all of the broken windows, mind you, just the one. Window repair, while not as expensive as say, a tear-off roof or a future child's therapy, was still around a couple hundred bucks a pop. So the first (non-picture window) window to hit the road was the one currently nailed shut with pink Styrofoam. In our minds, it was more affordable to repair and replace windows on a case by case basis. This was probably not exactly true in terms of cost effectiveness, but we really weren't letting that kind of rational thinking slow us down any longer.

The hardest part of this whole process was actually getting the contractor to the darned house. Unfortunately, we couldn't use the plate glass repair shop up the street (they of the stellar two-day turnaround) because they didn't sell and install normal household windows.

Regardless of the fact that I tried to convince them this was no normal household.

It had taken a few tries to get someone to quote us, because we kept running into the roadblock called "Did you speak with Monica, or someone else?"

I'm not sure who this magical entity named Monica was, but if you wanted to meet with someone before speaking to her- forget it! She was apparently the only one with access to the appointment book, the contractors' phone numbers, and the computer password. God bless Monica.

There was the initial consult. There was some measuring. (Done by "their guy. Everyone always has their own "guy." This

I have learned. Maybe Monica *is* their guy?) Then there was the actual installation of the windows. I was so excited that I just sort of hovered in the corner and prayed that I wouldn't pee out of joy. (Or incontinence.) And you know what? Not one thing went wrong with the removal of that mess and subsequent installation of a sparkly new window (which opened and closed and didn't even have any pink foam on it *anywhere*). Sure, they were two hours later than their scheduled time, but I had realized that that was rather par for the course. Late Show *way* trumps No Show. Especially when they do their job well. Because there were no cautionary tales of broken glass, drunken contractors, or gaping holes in the wall. Just…a window that opened and closed and looked exactly like a window ought to look.

That evening, P.J. returned home to find a bedroom out of a magazine. That is, if he squinted his eyes really hard. And defined "magazine" as "lesser quality brochure." The bed was pushed against the shiny new window and was made up with quilts and throw pillows of a vaguely Moroccan color scheme. (We could do that now, the whole "making the bed" thing, since we now possessed the key element.)

Amber lamps glowed from their new perches atop bedside tables which, again, were facilitated by the positioning of an actual bed. Secondhand curtains of sage green silk hung from the tops of the newly sanded windows and looked rather fabulous in the early evening light.

I mean, sure, the screws holding up the curtain hooks weren't exactly secured "properly," but that could easily be remedied as soon as I remembered to charge the power drill. Also, it occurred to me that most people don't necessarily hang curtain hooks on drywall screws. At least not when they're trying to be all fancy.

And yes, the curtains had a few patches of dark water stains (which is most likely why they were gifted to us in the first place), but as long as the sun wasn't shining directly through the curtains, I didn't feel like anyone would ever truly judge us.

Despite these smallish design flaws, the master bedroom had just become the nicest room in the house. P.J., ever-wise, threw an arm around my shoulder and acknowledged that he didn't deserve me.

We both took a minute to pretend that was true.

A note on general contractors: the majority of them, for some bizarrely archaic reason, still believe that the point person in any household is The Man. Or, more condescendingly, The Husband.

I've had folks ask to speak to my husband on numerous occasions, usually before they even know my marital status. Will he be present for the free consultation? Can we have his number as a backup? Do you fix him meatloaf after fetching his slippers?

This strikes me as terribly odd, funny, or angering, depending on my mood. Here are the facts, Jack: we- my husband *and* I- own a home that could potentially rack you up hundreds of thousands of billable hours (if I have my way), or at the very least enough hours to "do something nice for fairly cheap" with the dilapidated second kitchen (if my husband has *his* way). The potential for remodel, reroute, redo, and reconfigure is staggering. So the one you really need to make nice with is the lady scheduling the appointment, meeting for the initial consult, following up with emailed questions, and ultimately deciding whom she wants to see on a day-in, day-out basis for the duration of the project.

And she ain't The Husband.

P.J. eventually had to cede contractor control to me after one too many snafus with a guy of his own selection; the guy would run into unexpected job issues, he'd ask to speak to P.J., I'd remind him that I could answer any questions about my homestead, he'd oversimplify the problem, I'd give a misinformed summary to my husband, P.J. would call the contractor, they'd discuss things on their own, the contractor would smile smugly at me the following day, and then I'd have to shoot him in the face.

So I found myself choosing to use companies and contractors who treated me as the

person hiring them- and not just as the Little Lady. Sometimes these choices were even made despite other companies' better

Yelp and Angie's List reviews.

I chose a mold removal guy because, on the follow up call, he remembered how far along I was in the pregnancy. (He did a totally fantastic job on the walls, incidentally.)

We eventually found a nice mix of fellows who would respectfully and promptly fix our home's current issues and, for their pains, receive a frighteningly large check.

But there were many (*many*) more things wrong with the house. And, as my Dad always told me, leave plumbing and electrical to the professionals. (I added a few other things to that list since buying this place. Like sheetrock! And anything involving a box cutter!) There'd be no way to find those types of professionals without copious amounts of trial and error and more Little Ladydom.

It was a tough pill to swallow.

But, like anything else, a tough pill is made easier by a nice, healthy gulp of coconut milkshake from the 24/7 diner down the street. Which one's husband so lovingly offers to procure after one's heating and cooling guy reminds the wife that "P.J. knows what I'm talking about. I'll talk to *him*."

What irritated me the most (on a lengthy list) about the folks working on our house was this: no one ever seemed to know what the heck they were talking about. (Even when P.J.

asked the question.) I got the sneaking suspicion that my electrician would say anything I wanted to hear that would just shut me up. Another contractor wanted to keep me from crying. And a third (and fourth and fifth) was simply a pathological liar trying to make a sale.

There were many times when, after a job was completed, P.J. and I would be poking around the job site only to discover a visible leak. A wall crack that let in sunlight. Or absolutely no abatement of *that flipping horrific smell*. We'd point these things out to the men whom we had already paid, and they'd say helpful things like, "Oh, a leak/crack/smell? We must have missed that. No problem."

This did nothing to ease the stinging knowledge that a) no one else in the universe cared about our home besides us, b) professionals make mistakes *all the time*, and c) they would definitely attempt to roll further repairs into our already whopping bill.

I resolved to stay vigilant on all aspects of who was doing what to this place. Which meant literally nothing, because I had no power whatsoever. None. Because they could start telling me that there were squirrels in tinfoil hats affecting the heat output *and I'd have no choice but to agree with them.*

Besides, for all of my complaints about the guys working on our house, I'm sure it had nothing on the dossier that the city of Chicago's union workers were putting together on me. ("She cries an awful lot. And smells like onions.")

During these months, the cats were really unhappy with us. They barely knew where they were. They took issue with men working on the windows and anything else needing repair; i.e., everything that had previously been attached to the house. And they showed their displeasure by scurrying like their tails were afire, beating the junk out of each other, and yowling like irate tween girls.

Unfortunately, on the sliding scale of importance, it read something like this: things upon which to rest, windows for air, cats' feelings.

And again, I thought my cats were great. Still do. But a line in the sand/litter had to be drawn somewhere.

Once we had a working bed and at least one good window, I think we got cocky. How else could you explain the pressing need to bring *more* stuff into the house?

A friend had given us a humongous filing cabinet before an out of state move. Being that a filing cabinet is one of those pieces for which you really need a good location (preferably before bringing the monolithic thing into the house) and being that we *didn't* have such a locale, it lived in the downstairs family room for a good month. At a right angle to the couch and next to a pile of things for the baby, because nothing says Family Time like a sharp metal drawer beaning your infant in the head.

We also didn't need a new couch for the living room. But there we were, Needing A New Couch on Craigslist. Sure, the upstairs had a gaping lack of furniture and places to sit, but I wasn't entirely sure that buying something was going to be the answer.

We found a great dark brown sectional. Ridiculously cheap, too. That should've been a clue. The guy had even said he'd drop it off, which was terrific. I didn't think the Passat was up for it, nor did P.J. want either of us renting and driving a U-Haul for one couch. (Although, wouldn't seeing a ginormous pregnant lady hop down from the cab of a truck be worth the price of admission?)

That night, a guy in his early twenties drove the couch over to our place and unloaded the sectional, which had been stashed in two pieces in the back of a large van. The first piece easily slid through the front door and was plopped into the front room.

Happily, I sat there to await the second half.

It would be a bit.

The second piece, containing a bit more of the L shape of the sectional, proved difficult to navigate through the front door and around the corner of the narrow foyer. (Had this house previously been inhabited by stick figures?) After about a half hour of attempting to get this thing in the house, the seller announced that he had a gig.

So, uh, 'bye.

P.J. and I stared at the piece currently wedged through the front door for a little while. Was it really that noticeable? Yeah, we'd probably have to get it the rest of the way inside the house.

Thankfully, at that very moment a couple of neighbors were walking by our house. They were either coming from or heading to the bar on the corner. (This nugget of info is more crucial than you'd think.) Neither of them spoke much English; actually, that's not fair to say. One had so-so English but the other was drunk beyond comprehension in any language.

Even with the new helpers, the couch failed to make it through the doorframe. The superbly drunk fellow decided to keep on shoving however, and through either the failed hearing of the elderly or the extreme inebriation of the ragingly drunk, he managed to disregard our cries of "Basta!" and thwacked the hinge of the door clean off with the arm of the couch.

So. No interior couch and no exterior door. Check.

We brought it around to the other side of the house to try the side door. And by "we," I mean "they." The only part *I* played in this three act drama was to wring my hands and crave tacos. Everyone else present shoved the couch through the door, up the stairs, and met resistance with the freakishly small angle of the hallway. At this point it was getting pretty late. Our neighbors helped us prop it against the third floor stairwell (a way station for misfit furniture; it must've heard that there had been a recent vacancy) and held out their hands, purportedly for payment.

P.J. lamely explained that we had given all of our cash to the couch guy, which solidified the idea that the new white neighbors were independently wealthy. So P.J., feeling guilty, offered them a six pack of beer.

They happily accepted.

We later found out from the elderly man's son-in-law that the man to whom we gifted beer was a serious alcoholic. This information was offered up rather accusingly, like we secretly wished to have *more* people puking on our railing. You've figured us out, *neighbor*.

We apologized anyhow.

For the next month, P.J. had the swell task of hoisting my large frame over the arm of the couch to get upstairs. At least it was a shorter height over which to heft than the box spring had been.

Did you know that pregnant women are heavier when they cry?

P.J. went back to Craigslist and found a guy who owned a completely legitimate business of sawing furniture in half and sewing them up once they were in their rightful locations. Hiring these men was cheaper than the purchase of the couch itself, and provided way more instant gratification.

I was so thrilled to have a couch in a non-weird location

that I offered the man and his brother some tacos. It's true, I offered them P.J.'s portion of our dinner. (They declined.)

Sprawling on our newly-reunited couch halves in the living room, P.J. noticed a tiny cigarette burn in one of the cushions. He asked me if I minded.

I informed him that no, no I did not mind. For I had recently given much thought to taking up smoking, myself.

CHAPTER SIX

(The "G" Word.)

Let's talk about the "G" word for a moment.

Gentrification.

It's an ugly, ugly word that basically insinuates a desire to whitewash the neighborhood. For the record, that's not at *all* what we had wanted. One or two fewer people urinating directly on our front stoop, sure, but not an influx of whiteys.

The area where we had purchased our big ol' cave of wonders was definitely a changing neighborhood. A mix of Filipino, Mexican, and Lebanese, the area's cultural diversity was well represented in the form of some of the best restaurants I'd ever visited. And I knew for a fact that I was singlehandedly keeping the Tamale Lady in business.

Our neighborhood also hosted a rather large community of immigrants; some were citizens, some not so much. Virtually none of our neighbors spoke English, which for the most part was totally fine with us. Until we had to inquire (in pidgin Spanish) if anyone knew anything about said pool of urine by the mailbox. That made it tricky.

It was also tough to bridge the communication gap when we needed to detect why our next door neighbors insisted upon using our gate instead of their own to access our shared walkway, littering it with positively putrid cheap cigarettes. And

Dos Equis empties. And plastic bags that flew around our yard like so much tumbleweed. And half-eaten pitas. And gum wrappers, lottery tickets, and at least one used diaper.

Someone informed us that littering was an epidemic in Mexico City, and that the majority of our neighbors truly viewed throwing trash in the street as the city's issue to deal with. I really wasn't cool with chalking that up to cultural difference, but admitting out loud that I didn't like living in squalor seemed unfairly racist. P.J. took matters into his own (gloved) hands by walking up and down the street with a trash bag multiple times a week. Whether the gesture came off as altruistic or slightly community service-esque, he was definitely chuckled at from porches and deemed that *gringo loco*.

There was more gang violence than I'd normally be comfy with in an eight block radius (as my ideal amount of gang violence would be "none"), but folks chalked that up to City Life. Let's just say that our new Chicago neighborhood felt more City than our old Chicago block did.

We should've been more aware of the situation we were walking into, however. After all, the garage (sans door) had been hosting a colorful assortment of entrepreneurs for about a year prior to our arrival. And one night as we returned home, we found someone leaning against our (newly doored) garage. She leaned in as we approached and sassily asked what we needed.

To park our car, P.J. responded.

The gal suddenly became really busy looking for an earring on the ground. Had we seen her earring?

P.J. told her to tell her friends that this kinda thing didn't happen here anymore.

She had no idea what we were talking about. She was simply looking for an earring.

"Tell your friends that-" P.J. began again.

The girl left quickly. (Even without finding her earring.)

Our home was the victim of vandalism more frequently than we would've cared for, like slashed and stolen outdoor decor and alley gang tags. Then there was stuff that we initially *thought* was vandalism but was actually just the results of our neighbors' evening habits, like bodily fluid-splattered trash cans, broken empties in the alley, sometimes the neighbors themselves in various sleeping positions.

So P.J. got awfully good at removing graffiti, hosing things down, and carefully articulating Spanish phrases such as "It seems that you have- once again- fallen asleep against our chain link fence."

Now, before people get all up in arms about a young, yuppie-ish couple moving into a new neighborhood and demanding that the residents look and act like them, fear not.

We had our fair share of fun with our white neighbors,

too.

On one side of our property line we had the Filipino who hated us. But on the other side? A family with a 300lb nineteen year-old, whom we'll call Joe. He lived with his mother and aunt in a brick two-flat with a fenced backyard. Despite this yard divider, we were usually privy to screaming matches between various family members. And for the uninitiated, few can throw down at the drop of a hat like a kid with severe Asperger's (plus some other unidentifiable challenges) can throw down at the drop of a hat.

These shriek fests would take place throughout the day and night, usually peaking in severity right along our walkway or in the kitchen window directly facing ours. After they ended, Joe's favored hip hop would blare from his room.

Besides his music, Joe also had a penchant for impressively long (one-sided) conversations- but only for the ears of my husband. It didn't even matter whether or not P.J. was home.

Joe would wait.

On the stoop.

Occasionally calling in through the screen door, "Is he home yet?"

I'd yell back that, since Joe was sitting in front of the door, he'd be the first to know. Considering he didn't want to have much to do with me whenever P.J. wasn't around, our contact was pretty minimal for most of the summer.

He was mostly harmless, if extremely imposing and ridiculously patient. But when he discovered that I was pregnant and, being the relatively sheltered youth that he was, he wanted me to tell him all about everything. Suddenly, I was the equivalent of a rock star, the president, and someone who actually resided on the moon.

I would occasionally indulge him with stories over the fence of how we were fixing up the nursery (from Goth den to light and sunny) and, when prompted, where babies come from. (Heaven.)

Even with my newfound intrigue, he still pretty much left me alone. That is, until the day that he cornered me by my front gate and informed me that he'd never seen a "real" pregnant woman before. I nodded, even though I had no idea what I was agreeing to.

"Can I see your belly?"

And I don't know what came over me. Maybe it was a wave of sympathy because, despite the sharpness of his intellect, Joe had the emotional age and life experience of an eight year-old boy. So perhaps it was familiarity with that age set, and the knowledge that, yeah, a pregnant belly was an oddly cool thing.

I uncrossed my arms and pointed at my mid-section, which was currently straining through one of Target's finest maternity tank tops.

"That's really big."

"Yep."

"Are you sure you're not having that baby *tomorrow?*"

"Couple more months, actually."

"Wow. Because you're the biggest thing I've ever seen."

"Okie doke."

(For the record, being told that you're the largest thing *ever* by someone of that magnitude- well, it stings. It just stings.)

We stood like that for a few more moments, Joe staring at my belly and me staring at Joe, wondering if there was a time limit on viewings. Or if I should institute one. I mentally added that my list of pregnancy rules for which I had previously been unaware. (What a *learning* experience pregnancy was!)

My rambling thought process was interrupted by a huge, meaty hand grabbing my shirt and yanking it up past my navel.

"Can I see the belly skin?"

I smacked his hand down and took a step back. Joe looked confused and extremely saddened. For some inane reason, I felt like *I* had been the one in the wrong and wanted to leave on good terms.

"You can't touch my skin, Joe. I…have allergies. To things touching me."

He brightened.

"Me *too!*"

And without another word, he turned and walked back inside his house. That was the last we spoke about that. But from then on, I shouted my end of our conversations from the relative confinement of first floor windows.

Just like everyone else on the street.

In the early days of living in our neighborhood, we'd play a whimsical game called Neighborhood Watch. This activity consisted of falling asleep late in the evening, only to be awoken by an inexplicable noise on the street. We'd then prop our heads on our elbows by the window (which was acting as our headboard) and surreptitiously spy on the offenders. It was pretty high-stakes.

Who would find the hooligan first?

Would he/she still be engaged in a criminal act?

Please, God, don't let them see us seeing them!

In some neighborhoods, seeing people run is a sign of a something rather yuppie. Jogging signifies bourgeois. In good neighborhoods, sprinting was a leisurely activity. On our block, sprinting meant something real just went down. Sprinting meant dodging the po-po.

Occasionally we'd phone things into the police. Other times, we'd drift back to sleep, happy in the knowledge that the car with the hair-trigger alarm had been stolen once and for all.

This game continued until we moved the bed. We had discovered that it had been in the least Feng Shui-appropriate position of all. Windows by the head? Guess you want bad dreams and a weird flow of energy all night- and not just from the crazies on the street! And our feet had been facing the door which, as everybody knows, is the *Chinese Position Of Death*, as that's how the body is carried out of a room or something equally morbid. Obviously our bed needed to face the north wall, signifying...something else.

Once the bed had moved, however, we were way too tired/apathetic to Watch The Neighborhood. Getting up to confirm that, yep, *our block was not a great place to walk at night* was becoming a little too anticlimactic.

We hadn't wanted Mayberry. Okay, we had, but we were also realistic in terms of what we'd get in the city proper. We had really wanted *neighbors*. The kind that chat over fences in non-angry tones. The kind that toss a ball *with* their kids in the yard, and not *at* them through an open window. The kind that retrieve your mail while you're away- and not the kind that rip open envelopes to see if cash might be inside.

Basically, I wanted to live in a suburb. In the city.

I felt like the biggest faker as I walked around our neighborhood. I had known that this area wasn't so hot for property loveliness/personal safety when we moved in, but here I was; whining about ramshackle properties and turning my rings to the insides of my palms. And even though I knew for a fact that people were being mugged and robbed left and right up here, the act of just *assuming* it would happen to me made me feel like a terrible person. I became so paranoid about coming off as offensive that I stopped mentioning the state of affairs in our neighborhood to friends and family. Don't Rock The Boat Flynn, that was me.

This went on until I realized that my paranoia of offending was offensive in and of itself. To the best of my knowledge, public self-soiling and teenaged gang violence weren't the bastions of Mexican culture. Nor Filipino. Nor Lebanese. It was totally okay to hate these acts of societal implosion; the same way that my non-peeing, non-shooting Mexican, Filipino, and Lebanese neighbors did.

I felt better. Because now that I wasn't in danger of being a racist or classist, I was free to focus my rage on the real divide; Nice and Not Nice.

"Nice" included free spinach pies. Eye contact. Sitting on the stoop and attempting to converse.

The "not nice" list was slightly lengthier: Passersby ripping flowers from our front yard. A drive-by shooting at 6pm on a Tuesday. Vomiting against my side door. Incessant car alarms. *Good God, so much trash.*

This new divide really opened my eyes. Namely, it made me realize that white people hadn't corned the "nice" market at all on this block, especially when you considered the parents who stood idly by, smoking, while their four year-old humped a fire hydrant. Or the drunken overflow from the corner bar, crying at 3pm and fighting at 2am. Or the folks who would cut through the Walgreens parking lot and amble down our alley, looking for drugs. All white. There was an important lesson in equality here, and it rather depressed me.

So I went all Hippie Mantra on my neighbors: I'd be the change I wished to see in the world. So I decided to be nice and quiet. I would be nice; quiet, and I wouldn't hit my future children. I wouldn't beat people up, and I'd keep my feces to myself.

So far, I've held up *my* end of the bargain.

CHAPTER SEVEN

(Things not to say to pregnant women. Or anyone, really.)

Regardless of whatever socioeconomic hilarity was going down in my neighborhood, the baby-growing train was still zooming down the tracks. And people were really (loudly) taking notice.

Now, I'm no etiquette expert, but it seems like the mere sight of a pregnant woman gives people all sorts of free rein in which to insult the expectant mother. I did not expect *that*. People generally fell into two categories: The Circle Of Life Singers and The Death Sentencers. I am still not sure which is worse.

The Circlers extolled the beauty of. Every. Single. Thing. You. Do. Generally with a gratingly knowing smile. You have a craving? I remember those days. Peeing? *Ah*, yes- magical. And inevitably, these are the people with whom you find yourself surrounded during a particularly bad bout with queasiness, with nary a Triscuit in sight. Few things are worse than nausea compounded with someone soothingly telling you what a blessing it is. A miracle. And how it will change your life. Forever.

If you're really unlucky, sometimes they'll cry at you.

This group also instinctively knows the Fingertip Touch, and they have neither fear nor social boundary keeping them from grazing this Touch across your belly, your forehead, your hair, your *boob*. It makes the skin crawl.

So does the Knowing Smile. Because here's the thing: when you're really feeling rotten during pregnancy, you certainly don't want anyone tempering your response, or telling you to be thankful.

Basically, all I wanted was for people to shake their heads in wonder and acknowledge how brave I was.

The Death Sentencers (closely related to the Just Waits) have their own formula for exhaustion. Cramping? You have no idea. Wait 'til *labor*. (Did I mention that I was in labor for 70 hours, they'll ask? They had to call in the Coast Guard.) Anything you've done, they've had it worse and are here to tell you how intensely awful every iota of pregnancy and labor will be for you. Because they know.

And it doesn't stop at labor and delivery, either. (Even though they know someone who died. Seriously. And so did their baby. Come to think of it, they were carrying their kid *just like you*.) These fine folks will be the first to tell you that they haven't slept in six years. Their niece had the worst colic ever recorded in the continental U.S. They have a friend with a baby that had an allergy to wool and *died*. Their gift to you is that of knowledge. This is the only thing I can imagine. I suppose it would be unfair to let a pregnant woman start a new chapter of her life with optimistic thoughts and a good outlook. Where's the life lesson in that?

For example: I'm about to hit you in the face with this Louisville slugger. It's really gonna hurt. In fact, you might die from it. Someone I know actually did. Ready? Ready? Oh, and you won't be able to sleep or afford anything ever again because of it. Stand still!

"Enjoy it now" was a common chorus from the Just Waits and Death Sentencers. This statement could be flung at a pregnant woman for the most innocuous of situations. Eating at a diner? *Enjoy it now.* ("When I had my first kid, I didn't have time to eat for months…is that a Reuben? Lemme tell you about a woman I know who ate a Reuben and *died…*") Walking down the street? ("Oh, I envy you your freedom…")

It was kind of like telling a patient about to undergo foot surgery to get in his foot-stompin' now. I'm fairly certain that no person ever actually enjoyed any activity that a person pressed upon them due to time constraints. It's the Sunday evening activity before school starts up again that Monday morning. Being told to acknowledge the last of your freedom is a bit of a buzz kill. How about we let the woman eat her sandwich and then (sometime down the road in the middle of a pureed pea debacle) allow her the fondness of that memory?

"Welcome to my world" is another one that must stop. You are not the ambassador of my new waistline. This is not your duchy. If some people are to believed (and with loudness on their side, they just may persevere), their life is more trying than anyone else's ever. This phrase is generally bandied about by women with a toddler and another on the way. You know what *that* means, right? You can never top them. They will always be one kid ahead. After your upcoming awful labor, they'll be right there to tell you about teething, potty training and SAT scores. You must allow them to frighten you. They've got nothing to lose and another twenty minutes on the meter.

Then there are the conversations which stop you in your tracks and break your brain with lack of social graces. Like the woman who informed me that I must be carrying a girl, for girls take all of the mother's beauty during pregnancy. To be fair, I hadn't yet showered that day and was carrying a sack of tacos. But I wasn't exactly a troll.

Or the random guy at The Home Depot who sidled up next to me and demanded- exasperated- to know how much bigger I was gonna *get*. I was six months along. (Also, was this really a trying time for *him*?)

How about the lady who guessed that I was having a boy because I was too humongous and out to *here*, and everyone knew that girls are carried lower. I actually apologized for my crazy weight gain. Again, I may have been holding some tacos.

Even well-meaning friends were making me cry, like the one who emailed me a story about a cat getting pregnant *while the cat was already pregnant*. I had long passed the point where the news brought me joy. I also made the executive decision to keep my husband away from me. (Unless he was bearing food.)

I almost broke when a stay-at-home Mom vocally

considered me "so lucky" for having a job as "relaxing" as nannying during my pregnancy. I mean, *come on*. I'm not a forklift operator, but fluffing pillows and (legally) downloading Enya would be relaxing uses of my time while pregnant. Extracting a kid from the top of the monkey bars ain't Zen.

I got rather good at nodding and smiling and hearing the strains of *Rocky Raccoon* whenever folks decided to educate me. I'm not entirely sure while I chose *Rocky Raccoon*. Possibly because it's impossible to think mind daggers at someone while recalling such a lyrically interesting song. By the time I got to the part about McGill who called herself Lil, I felt much better about life.

I did make one rookie error in front of this group, however. A huge one.

Even before anyone knew the gender of our baby (even before the baby *had* a gender), we spilled on the kid's name. To be fair, we were really excited. Also, P.J. and I had decided on the girl's name before we had been dating for a full year and the boy's name by the time we got married.

Our girl's first name would be the same as my favorite Golden Era cinema heroine and would have P.J.'s grandmother's name for her middle. Our boy would be named after my great-grandfather and his middle name would be a family name from P.J.'s side. We felt good about these choices. Fabulous, in fact, and couldn't imagine any more perfect names for our beloved fetus; especially by the time came around for us to actually name someone.

But boy, did we not expect everyone else's feelings on this matter. Regardless of the fact that no one else really needed a say in this discussion, turns out that everyone else still really got to Have Their Say.

The girl's name was too cutesy.

And too dusty.

Or, it was just perfect. But the boy's name was weird.

And a little "eh."

It was also rather dusty.

And why aren't you naming her after someone in *your* family?

Is that really a family name on his side?

I like the name Madeline. You should name her Madeline.

And so forth.

It was bizarre. If we had waited to reveal the name, everyone (even the haters) would've had to suck it up and smile politely at the news. Because it takes a pretty junky person to look at a newborn child and announce, "I knew a Chad in high school. He was such a *jerk*."

No. You look at that new little Chad and declare that he will become the new standard for all future Chads.

When expectant parents finally hit upon that one perfect name, there's this feeling of *yes*, this is it! Every single person who hears it and comes into contact with not only his name *but our baby himself* will be refreshed and slightly envious of our choices! It will strike that subtle balance between trendy, timeless, and painfully cool- without being weird. This name will represent a part of our history, and also pave the way for this kid's imminently impressive future. It'll be cute enough that a clothing boutique could be named after him, yet he could still have a non-embarrassing moniker for his law practice.

But let's be honest. The chances of even a small cross-section of *people you know* liking this future baby's name is quite small. The rest of the population will roll their eyes and have one of these two thoughts:

-Do you have even an ounce of originality at all?

-Naming your kid after a noun doesn't signify your youth.

There is no way in the history of ways that every single person you meet will agree upon one favorable name for your baby. It's even less likely that'll it be the name you choose. But as long as you steer clear of embarrassing initials and give full acknowledgement to even the slightest thought of "Hey, this might be a cruel thing to do to someone I purportedly love," then I say you should go for it. After all, *you* might as well like your kid's name.

After enduring a lot of negativity and odd comments, I finally got to the point where I wanted to ask how many children *they* had had and how the whole naming of their own offspring thing had worked out for them. Or if they didn't have any, maybe they could hurry up and name their own darned kids something terrific.

Even though I totally had a dog with that name. He peed all over the place. Then he died.

Despite the fact that we had no idea whether we were expecting a baby boy or girl, I was fairly certain the child I carried was a dude. There was no scientific evidence to back this up. Just Mother's Intuition, something that I was repeatedly informed was Never Wrong.

Roughly half of the people polled stated that I *looked* like I was having a boy, whatever the heck that meant. For some folks, it meant I was carrying low and out front. For others, it was definitely because my belly looked like a basketball. And still others told me I was way up high, a positive Boy indicator. All I took away from these conversations was that it was *for sure* a boy and, however you looked at it (or me), I was visibly and conversationally pregnant.

Such an amount of completely random women in public couldn't possibly be wrong. It obviously signified a boy.

Or a girl.

Then there were my dreams. Loads of them. In every single one I was handed a healthy, squalling little boy. Nary one baby girl. And, as I've been lucky enough to have had nightly vivid dreams since childhood, I put a lot of stock into dreams.

Or I could've been snacking way too close to bedtime.

At this point in the pregnancy, my doctor suggested that I might need a C-section, due to the kiddo's breech position right up under my lung and ribcage. This possibility brought on its own panics and concerns and, of course, a chorus of comments from the peanut gallery.

Again, I got the So Lucky platitudes. My thought was-really? Major abdominal surgery is a prize? What kind of crappy lottery did *I* win? Neither delivery option seemed like a stroll by the seaside, but I certainly wasn't clapping my hands at the idea of a ninety inch needle jabbing my spinal column. (My mind did momentarily enjoy the vision of a morphine drip, however.) The other side of that coin was the group who told me *not* to have a C-section, regardless of what the doctor *may have been telling me*. Because doctors have Agendas. And my body Knows What It's Doing.

Not for the first time, I realized that people really enjoy speaking at people. And even the most well-meaning passerby will tell you about your specific pregnancy simply to validate their own choices. I contemplated marketing pregnancy earplugs.

The only people who can get away with saying outrageous things to a pregnant woman are children. They can make even the biggest insult seem downright charming and worthy of tweeting.

Although that might not be the loftiest of standards, for I've been known to tweet about what shape I had cut into my sandwich. (Usually a heart, for the record.)

One of my toddler charges grabbed one of my breasts one afternoon and asked if *those* were babies, too. When I explained that no, that was my chest and she had one as well, she laughed. (A lot.) She said that they were too big to be "a chest," and she'd never have one of *those*. Then she laughed some more. I laughed as well, even though it wasn't funny at all.

I didn't want to seem like a bad sport.

However, we had bigger fish to fry than a child's mockery of my figure.

The same plumber we had used when replacing the ancient boiler and defunct water heater had recently returned to bleed the valves and, while there, replace a radiator endcap. These baseboard radiators were completely warped and rather unattractive floor units but, since they worked, were extremely low on the list of things to replace in the next ten years.

Our plumber assured us that they could replicate the missing endcap, but that his guy would need to take the existing cap back with him that day. We had no problem with this. None at all.

Until his guy, Johnny, decided to go AWOL on the job

and was never heard from again. This was sad for many reasons. Among them, he was a good plumber who knew well the wonkiness of our home and he did a fairly good job of not gouging our wallets for relatively simple procedures.

It was also sad because Johnny still had our radiator endcap and wasn't returning any calls. Now we were out *two* endcaps.

Not the end of the world by any stretch, but it certainly meant that we now had a hole on either side of our floor heater. And it seemed a little unfair. Our house had plenty of holes already, thankyouverymuch. A new and completely random one was just a little insulting.

When the plumber realized that Johnny was gone for good, they came back to our house and borrowed another endcap- this time from the kitchen radiator. (I kinda wanted to write my name inside of it in Sharpie.)

But, within weeks, all of our ugly heating units were properly capped with matching warped metal of their own. We were borderline happy with the status quo of an unattractive corner of the house.

We were less happy when the plumber tried to charge us for four endcaps.

Forget the Ivy League; I decided then and there that this unborn baby would be heading to Trade School as soon as possible.

By the beginning of my third trimester, I was feeling like less of an Earth Mother and more of an Aging Rocky.

And despite my best Pilates intentions, I wasn't exactly feeling ready for my imaginary photo shoot. Turns out, unless you're a super demon pregnant woman who runs marathons and eats and eats and *doesn't gain a bit, it's so annoying, I eat all day long*, you're going to pack on at least some baby weight.

Also, if you're in the former category, I already resent you. Yes, I said it.

I had gained all of the weight that had been recommended for someone of my size and frame. But that didn't stop me from gaining. An actual conversation with my O.B. went like this:

O.B.: You're a little over what your weight should *be* at this point. And you've still got ten weeks left to go.

Me: Should I diet? Start eating just melon?

O.B.: No way. Restricting calories would be unhealthy for the baby.

Me: So…I should just feel badly? Stress about it?

He suggested that I remain "mindful" of my weight gain. Which just may be the least helpful thing any man has ever said to me, ever, followed closely by that dude's remark at The Home Depot.

As a recovering actress, it was an unbelievably difficult

concept to wrap one's head around. (Namely mine.) The idea of having to gain weight- but not *too much*- initially made me sad and concerned. Then it made me hungry. And a little while after that, I couldn't even manage the appropriate angst, chalking each new pound under the Easily Lost After The Baby Comes category. (Which is totally a doable plan. I highly recommend.)

It probably didn't help that, each time I ran into a friend, I would get the usual belly-grab and the exclaimed "I can't believe how *huge* you are!" Sometimes I would literally run into them; something about objects in motion or pendulums.

Regardless, the "huge" thing is awful to say to anyone, not matter how many people they're currently carrying inside of their organs. Because honestly, the further along in pregnancy a woman is, the more fervently she hopes that she *doesn't* look massive. And when you affirm that, yes, she's rather large, you just know she's going to stalk some unwitting taco joint, which will only make the problem worse.

P.J. and I invented a term for why people couldn't handle seeing me so gigantic. We called it Hollywood Pregnancy. Movies and TV are notorious for showing women who are purportedly in their third trimester, but who only feature the cutest of tiny baby bumps. A hand on the lower back to start labor, a minor scream fest, and then they're handed an infant who has already aged roughly six months.

I think I reached *my* Hollywood Pregnancy around month four or five. After that, the proportions of my belly reached such widths and heights that it truly horrified the sensibilities of the uninformed masses. I could hardly blame them (outwardly), because it terrified me daily as well.

Injured pride notwithstanding, I was also losing my marbles due to waking up to pee. And waking up *not* to pee. I had never been the stillest of sleepers, but now couldn't even manage a twenty minute stretch without becoming aware of my full bladder, *stomped* bladder, cramps and spasms akin to having calf muscles ripped out of my legs with a penknife, and extreme guilt at having kicked my husband in the ribs. (Again.) Though how I managed that while propped between body pillows, leg pillows and a neck support crammed under my lower back to keep me firmly on my side is anyone's guess.

Jumping (safely) back to Fashion; at this point in the pregnancy I'd have happily taken those animal patterns and cutesy prints- if they'd still fit. And of course, by now it was late summer, a prime season for weddings, beach events, and clothing a bit more involved than elastic shorts with the waistband rolled down five times. I made do with dresses resembling togas and anything with little belts around the ribcage, allowing for delineation.

And may I make a swimsuit recommendation? Avoid checkered prints. Even if the thing somehow manages to fit the girth of your boobs and belly, you're still going to look like an unfortunate tablecloth. This is not an idle suggestion. I have the photographic proof. (And the food stains.)

There were so many more changes that happened to my body at this stage in the pregnancy; among them something that Judy Blume had *never* imagined writing into chapter books: Early lactation. Now, I definitely knew how a nursing mother feeds her child. I attended LAMO, after all. (It was a mandatory elementary school class which stood for Learning About Myself And Others. I always felt that this should have been called LAMAO, even though the rest of the fifth grade class referred to it as LAME-O. Kids are so funny.) However, they really never touched upon that all-too-terrifying moment when the occasional droplet of milk would emerge from a nipple with nary a child in sight. We're not talking a deluge, here, and in fact so paltry an amount that it could easily be explained away as errant take out spills. (For example.)

But the very first time it happened to me in the third trimester I was fairly certain that I was dying. Something was coming out of a part that had never done anything of the sort before and it made me feel rather like my body was now (even more) part alien. P.J. was not as sympathetic as I might have hoped. In fact, he thought it was insanely cool and asked if he could see. I was shocked that he'd want to witness firsthand symptoms of my terrifying demise.

But one benefit to being this hugely pregnant was that my nails and hair had become fully fabulous. Long, strong, thick and healthy, this could have been a serious plus for me, beauty-wise.

Too bad I was feeling too chubby, paranoid about my tank top, and full of tears to appreciate my stellar ponytail.

CHAPTER EIGHT

(Higher Education, or, Are These People High?)

I'll admit it. I went into the childbirth classes thinking that I was ahead of the curve. These were the classes formerly known as Lamaze, but now which encompassed every birth technique shy of standing on one's head and *thinking* the child out. (Note: This is not an option. Trust me.)

Going by the brochures alone, a bunch of these classes seemed to concern breathing (at which I was already awesome) and keeping the kid alive (for which I had at least eight miniature testimonials).

But we went to Great Expectations. Mainly because we felt like if we didn't go, the hospital would somehow be alerted and we wouldn't get to keep the baby. And after all the work we had (kinda) put into the house, it just wouldn't have seemed right.

And what a mixed bowl of party nuts we found there! Ten couples, all arranged in a circle in order of due dates. Of course, I discovered that nugget of information right after I had already made myself comfy on a yoga ball and didn't much feel like moving two couples to the right, thanks so much. But I did it anyway. Good Little Follower Flynn, reporting for duty.

I found myself eyeing the women to my left and right, wondering if I looked bigger than the women due after me, yet hoping that I looked smaller than the women who were to come before me. It was like a sixth grade mixer and everyone was chubby. Even the popular girls.

P.J. reassured me that I was the least pregnant-looking girl in the room. Also, any positive thoughts and feelings and hopes I could possibly be having were all true, whatever they were. (Where was *he* when I was in middle school?)

Next we introduced ourselves and announced our birth plans. This, surprisingly enough, was just about as warmly received as facing a firing squad. Turns out, if you like drugs, *you hate your child*. If you choose to go au natural, *you hate yourself. And are downright insane.* Every single parental choice was met with a cocked eyebrow and an expression that read: Really? Poor thing.

It started us off on the right foot and really set the tone for sharing.

Onward to: videos of women laboring their ways through natural childbirth! At this point, I barely wanted to be a part of my *own* special process, let alone stare down the barrel of some (unshaven) woman's questionable birth plan. One unfortunate gal featured in the video didn't speak English, seemed to be laboring solo, didn't fully understand that there wouldn't be an epidural involved, and wasn't quite sure what the whole "filming" thing meant.

Her postpartum interview was akin to that of a shell-shocked tornado victim. I really felt for her.

Another woman brought what we termed her Labor

Headband and was there to Make. This. Thing. Happen. We felt that the headband deserved its own spinoff series. Too bad for her that, along with the headband, she possessed a whiny demeanor, a useless husband, and the worst labor face I've ever seen in all of my years watching TLC and various birth stories.

I understand that no one's there to win a beauty contest, but the woman's mug seriously seemed to say This Is What I've Practiced And Think I Should Look Like. (This could be unfair of me, I realize.)

As for the useless husband? As she did her thing, he kept patting her and (gratingly) murmuring "You're doing great. Great. You're doing real great. Great." Like Rain Man in scrubs.

During the labor, he even took a break to tell the camera how tired he was. P.J. and I both wanted to flick that couple in their collective eye.

However, something we could not begrudge them in their post-baby interview; the lower level of their home was completely finished and *gorgeous*.

After the video portion of the class had ended, we got to try out our own contractions! The husbands were able to squeeze their partner's body part and help their spouse breathe through it. Any ol' part they chose. Most guys chose the upper arm, but my husband grabbed my thigh and gave it a vice-like grip. (He's a good student and really wanted the teacher to notice this fact.) Since I'm rather ticklish, I began to laugh. P.J.

compensated by switching it up and rubbing my thigh like a good labor coach. I swatted his hand away and yelped at the charley horse he was causing.

The teacher popped an aspirin.

At the end of that class, I felt fully non-ready to labor naturally. Ever.

The next week was Epidural Night! (Nothing like Taco Night. At all.) We got to see some of the best over-actors in the business scream in pain until the miracle of hypodermic needles entered the stage.

My favorite video moment concerned a lady who shrieked in agony until her doctor appeared, whereupon she promptly stopped. She brushed some hair from her face (where was *her* headband?) and asked the doctor if the needle would hurt. Like she was asking how often the #78 bus came this way. The doctor promised her it would only be a small pinch. A bee sting, really. I wanted to pipe in that it couldn't possibly be any worse than the demon she had previously been attempting to exorcise from her nether regions.

They also shoved a C-section video all up in there. I was not okay with that. My feelings regarding C-sections were thus: They would not need my help. I wouldn't even be allowed to see past the makeshift tent! I, in fact, would not care to know what organs of mine were being placed on which trays, nor would I wish to know how many layers of whatever they would be peeling back with skin clamps. Too much knowledge seemed cruel.

And really, really gross.

There was also an animated short (*not* featuring Mortimer Mouse or anyone halfway amusing) but instead was a lighthearted look at the layers of muscle and tissue that are necessary to fillet in an average C-section. Not okay. Again, unless you expect me to perform one of these jobbies on myself, let's go for the Less Is More school of thought. The voiceover suggested that if a patient were to feel anxious about this procedure (maybe they were forced to watch the videos?) perhaps having her doctor explain it to her in these terms would ease some stress.

I filed away that bit of Helpful Knowledge.

Also, there was a nugget of info that claimed a baby could be removed from the uterus within five minutes of the first incision. *Five minutes.* That seemed an awful lot like needless bragging to me.

"Take your time, friend," I planned on telling my surgeon. "Let's not rush this."

P.J. suggested that this video was tossed in there as an It's Not *So* Bad consolation prize. All I came away with was the image of a woman, strapped down on the bed with her arms in a T, being rotated like a pig on a spit either for circulation's sake (or just the nurses' amusement), who was threatening to vomit at any minute.

Heck of a prize. Wonder what the other contestants got?

There was a touching moment towards the end wherein the mother got to blink in the general direction of her newborn, nuzzle him with her numbed chin, and promise to hold him in roughly an hour and a half.

We followed up these hard-hitting dramas with a breezy clip from the Hugh Grant and Julianne Moore comedic romp *Nine Months*. The scene was the one where Robin Williams- ever the affable doc- bungled the check-in for the heavily laboring Moore, leading Grant to somehow shove his wheelchair-bound wife into an open elevator. The RN leading our class quipped that that was *not* how to go into labor.

I kid you not.

Ending the class with a little yoga and pretend contractions while rolling myself over a large ball was fun, too. And I'm pretty sure that we're in trouble if I have to include the labor method of looking deeply into my spouse's eyes. He's really funny. Especially when he's Trying To Be Serious. I assured him that there would be no teachers to impress in the delivery room. I think he was ready to change partners.

At the end of *this* class, I was quite certain that I didn't want an epidural, either.

Nor a C-section.

This left me with the option of being gently nudged awake and handed the baby I had somehow (painlessly) had in my slumber.

I liked that one.

We got to come back again for Infant First-Aid and CPR Night. Now, regardless of the fact that this exact knowledge had been a job requirement of mine since 2002, the idea of having to perform any such thing on *my* child was enough to make me sweat. (Good thing I had recently been given a labor headband of my own. No flyaways!)

Each couple was handed a fake-yet-creepily-realistic baby over which to panic. Ours was a darling little black baby with an unfortunately twisted air pipe. This served to make us look like morons. ("Blow *in* his mouth." "I *am*!") Our defective baby was whisked away and replaced with a healthy fake baby. Which I'm pretty sure is not representative of any actual Having A Child scenario.

Having proven that we could beat on a pretend kid's chest and keep his heart going to the tune of Stayin' Alive, we were ready for some video.

Our DVD host, a grinning coke addict of a woman, was more than ready to tell us how easily our kid could just up and die. Anywhere. Really, at any moment, regardless of how vigilant we were being. Even though we could never possibly watch him every second. Like, had you ever realized that your baby could just stop breathing? And the danger didn't end with your own children. I bet you hadn't planned for the possibility of being at a family picnic and having your Dad fall over. Or even while playing Nintendo with friends and eating pizza, someone could choke. And die.

Given these cripplingly scary and rather alarmist scenarios, we were comforted by the actors ready to show us what to do. Except (and I'm not entirely sure why) they were clad in matching track suits. Perhaps to speed up their response time? But that's not realistic for my lifestyle. How about a gal in a hoodie and jeans? Maybe some impractical espadrilles? Regardless, videos of the matchy-matchys were what we got, standing in front of walls draped with sheets.

And they were *intense*. (The portrayals, I mean. The sheets were so-so.)

These folks, upon finding a track-suit clad victim (one of their own!) lying motionless on the ground, got to really stretch their acting muscles and call out *to no one* to dial 911. This was after they poked the lifeless form at their feet with a cursory "Hey, You."

One Asian girl was completely devoid of emotion or inflection. I did not believe for a minute that she cared whether her scene partner lived or died. A large black gal, on the other hand, screamed for help at a "passerby" with such force that I actually reached for my cell. Can we choose which Good Samaritan stumbles upon our non-breathing bodies? I'd pick her.

Another random informational nugget hit us out of the blue: Did you know you should only try to remove a food blockage if it is immediately visible? Our host demonstrated this by gently taking an M&M out from between the lips of a mannequin. Now, I don't exactly have a track suit; but where I'm from, that's not called "choking." That's called "eating an M&M."

My favorite part of the evening came at the end of show when our tweaked narrator proudly informed us that we "now have all the tools we need to save lives…just like Gary."

This freaked me out. How did I miss Gary? Was he in one of the track suits? Maybe the Dad who keeled over in the backyard?

Talk about ending on a cliffhanger.

Our class even got to take a field trip. Right up to the maternity and delivery wards to poke around rooms like it was real estate. ("Honey, do you see this wood trim? Classy!") The rooms boasted the ability to turn from a mini operating room into the place where you, your husband, and infant would Not Sleep until you got to go home. (To Not Sleep there.) We all nodded and smiled appropriately, but seriously; it's not like we were auditioning other places in which to be wearing our headbands.

I did, however, take small comfort in the fact that everything happened in one room. It lessened the sheer numbers of people who would have to accidentally see me naked than if I were thrust from room to room. (Look, I've seen the videos.)

On our way out, we passed a shell-shocked woman being pushed in a wheelchair. She was holding the tiniest bundle of blankies and being followed at a distance by her dazed husband. Her nurse benevolently whispered that *yesterday* she had been just like *us*!

I had no wish to ever know what sort of trauma that poor soul had just undergone.

All too soon it was our last night of Great Expectations, at which point I fervently believed that the class should've been renamed Eh…A Baby?

The last night was Scare The Parents Night. (The least like Taco Night of any of them.) Not only could one's child just up and stop breathing, as we had so recently learned, but a whole host of other issues could just spring up once we were legally in charge of this new kid. (Which, apparently, happens *immediately*. Who okayed that one? Don't you at least need a recommendation? Didn't you see my twisty-piped African American child?)

SIDS was a particularly cruel topic. Okay, so, there's *no* way to predict it, there are *no* warning signs, and even though the mother could be ever-vigilant, the baby could just *die*? Yes, but as long as you put the baby to bed- naked- on its back and place nothing within a twenty foot radius of her (save for a few industrial strength fans for air circulation) you can say you tried.

No wonder some women descend into panic. There is literally no end to the laundry list of worries. That's why we were also alerted about our own exhaustion, mood swings, pain, and anxieties. This part frightened me. For I already felt this way, with more than a month to go. And, as we were informed, these symptoms occur in Moms who "care too much."

Which sounded to me like a healthy dose of neglect would be better for every single person involved, especially the frozen and lonely infant wondering what a lovie was.

I had already had it up to my bloodshot eyeballs with parental scare tactics during my time as a nanny. The baby product recalls because of injuries and deaths were the worst. Horrifying? Yes. Preventable? I'll hazard a guess and say absolutely.

Especially the drop-side crib ban after some rails plummeted to the ground. *After being installed incorrectly.* I liken that to suing the makers of my car after a kid falls out of it (after I left the doors open).

Or the wagon recall because- ready for it?- a few kids toppled out and got banged up. Unless we're talking about the Oregon Trail, wagons do not come with covered roofs, and some of those stories sounded suspiciously like *kids playing with a wagon*.

And the fact that one can no longer buy any medicine other than Tylenol for a child under the age of four. Granted, there are very few occasions where things other than vapo-rub or a good shower steaming are needed for a baby's cold, but to do away with it altogether? And simply because people were overdosing their kids? It reminds me of the time in second grade when one kid started talking during silent reading time, and we *all* had to put our heads on our desks in punishment. (That was a terrible day.)

Then there's the stroller parts recall because parents were pinching their kids' fingers in the stroller's hinges while folding up the contraption. How about, instead, we all just agree to remove the kids from the stroller before we try to collapse the thing?

And I completely believe in making things safe, chemical and BPA-free for little ones (I *did* go to a hippie school, after all, and had a fair bit of crunchiness absorbed through osmosis), but I'm also a big ol' proponent of Personal Responsibility. Are hoodie strings potentially dangerous? Absolutely. But you know what else is? *Not watching your toddler for any great length of time.* Granted, these were my thoughts prior to actually having a kid of my own. I was fully open to realizing how different safety issues could become once the kid was mine 24/7, but I was willing to bet that I wouldn't start being all litigation-happy.

(Unless it was a *real* moneymaker.)

But back to the last of our (Great) Expectations.

Lest you think that Scare The Parents Night was video-free, we got to see an incredibly detailed film concerning the circumcision procedure. To which I said: Come *on*. I am *definitely* not going to have to do *that* by my lonesome! This was followed up by watching medical professionals torture newborns with steroid eye drops and Vitamin K needles the size of Mir.

All of these Required By Law things being done to newborns made me long for the Wild West. Sure, the infant mortality rate was astronomical, but I bet *they* didn't have to watch this stuff.

I was so dazed by all of this imparted information that, by the time a goody bag was being passed around I had completely missed its purpose. Someone handed me the largest sanitary pad I had ever seen in my life and I thanked them, pocketing it. The weird stares I received made me wonder if I was supposed to share it. Turns out I was, as just moments later the teacher asked us to hold up our items for group discussion. (*Oh*.) Sure made a lot more sense why a guy across the room was clutching a humongous bottle of stool softener.

And that was it. We were now proud graduates of this class, ready to panic like experts at the prospect of having and keeping a baby within one short month.

We decided to review the CPR on a weekly basis, mainly for use on each other.

CHAPTER NINE

(She's REALLY pregnant, now; or First World Problems)

As the window on my childless, social life-free and panicky existence started to close, I prepared myself for the full of child (yet still social life-free and panicky) next phase of my existence.

I remember telling people that there wasn't enough *time*. I'm not entirely sure what I was doing besides taking informative classes and bawling at plaster holes in the ceilings, but in my mind I was *booked*. And I can say this to Past Me because I'm awfully close to the source: Just Wait. You think your theatre career is stalling *now*? You miss drinking *what* with your friends? (Answers: Yes. And sangria.)

My kid was still fully breech, in a position called "frank breech," in fact. (Frankly, your kid isn't going to flip. He's breech.) This solidified the idea of a C-section being the way to go, at least in my doctor's mind. I still wasn't too sure. I really hated needles, regardless of the severity in which I'd been poked, prodded, and probed up to this point. From what I learned in Great Expectations, a C-section was a big ol' Needlepalooza.

Also, I've read *MacBeth*. That whole "not born of woman" thing? It worried me.

The doctor was also gently suggesting that this child was already just shy of gigantic. This knowledge served the dual purpose of cementing the baby's right side-up (or, rather, wrong side-up) position, and also scaring the bejeezus out of me.

So I went back to the internet for tips other than "rest up" and "book your C-section." Here is what I came away with: Ice your belly. Eat crazy foods. Think flippy thoughts. Hang out upside down, against a couch.

Really good suggestions, all.

Except: It was darned hot out. The ice melted before it could serve its purpose (but still felt really good). I'd been cornering the market on crazy food-eatin' for close to eight months. I was plum out of flippy thoughts. And I've never even been able to manage that couch thing when *not* pregnant. Even with an ironing board for help. (That was an actual suggestion.) I can just see the tragic headline now: Area Heifer Offs Herself By Jackknifing Into Board; Seamless Couch Arm. (She Was Damp And Surrounded By Kale.)

I gave up on convincing my child to turn. I really couldn't blame the baby, after all. Neither P.J. nor I had ever learned how to successfully dive. Why were we expecting miracles from our offspring?

We had agreed to stop working on the house for the time being. This was half to give ourselves a mental break, and half to prevent me from falling on any more items of furniture. I wasn't thrilled about this, because there was still so much left to do. P.J. helpfully pointed out that there would be stuff left to do until our future child hit middle school. And while he had become increasingly strict about Leaving Tasks For Him To Do (For The Love Of God), he didn't say anything about nesting.

It became kind of like a game of poker: I see your Put That Down and raise you a Guess Which Cabinet Is Holding The Dishes Today?

Here is what the house looked like before I brought our child into the world:

The baby's nursery was as done as we could manage. The (potentially angering) Pale Sunshine walls had been slapped with a few more coats of paint which, while not entirely hiding streaks of maroon in certain lights, was a decently passable shade of mostly solid yellow. The window frames had been patched and sanded to the best of my ability, and the sloppy parts were hidden by charmingly gender-nonspecific curtains. All of the fabrics were golden and featured patterns of crayoned rainbow circles. Hand-knitted throws were artfully (for now) draped over a rocking chair. (I had a feeling that this would pave the way for hand-knitted throws being artfully thrown over the hamper, the diaper pail, and, occasionally, the baby.) A cherry red Ikea rug showcased a bear and a frog driving a wagon and a boat, respectively.

They were also clutching flags and balloons, which was

not exactly the type of vehicle behavior I would hope to impart to the baby, but "cute" way outranked "legal" by now.

Books were organized by height and color, something that I imagined wouldn't last too long into the kid's actual childhood, but which made my heart feel good. I mean, the baby's room still lacked an actual door and working doorframe, so I took whatever illusions of order I could get.

A cozy bassinet lived right across the hall in the master bedroom which, for its part, didn't possess a doorframe of its own either. It was a decent semblance of a grownup's room however, with walls a deeper shade of gold than the baby's, windows which continued to open and close and work better than their foamy pink predecessors, and nary a slur of graffiti in sight.

The master bathroom was clean. And that's the best thing that could possibly be said about it. Even with all of the traces of blood-like residue removed, it still possessed a dingy sink, a medicine cabinet that threatened to plunge to the floor at any moment, and an old person's shower. You know the type; the plastic seat that's been fitted over an existing shower stall. Add a rickety shower door off of its hinge and voila: masterful bath.

The hallway had been painted an (immediately regretted) optical illusion paint called Victorian Pearl. This was the color we had chosen for all of the stairwells, the hallways, and the entirety of the kitchen. We bought so many cans of this one shade that we may actually be shareholders. And while it looked beige and boring and totally fine under the Home Depot light, the outdoor light, and the dimly lit hallway's light, the moment it dried it became a shade that can only be called pink. Soft, ballerina, That's An Awful Color For A Kitchen pink.

But it stayed, for now. *Because there was no more flipping time to repaint, goddammit- didn't you look at the color in the store? Yeah, but was I the one who chose it? No! No I was NOT.*

The best thing that could be said about the kitchen, aside from the recently shoved-in stainless steel appliances (and that was saying quite a bit), was that there were no longer holes in the dark green floor. Sure, the patched parts looked extremely patched, and P.J. never missed an opportunity to inform guests that I had patched *that* spot and *that* one (like it wouldn't be obvious that perhaps the new floor tiles were the mismatched leprechaun green ones). I told him to start leaving that out of the tour, because it seemed like a pity story. ("Well, she was down on the floor, anyhow. So she grouted.")

The thin, wooden cabinets were hanging on by a thread and the backsplash tiles were horrifically stained and more than a little dated. But since they were functional, they stayed. Also, the ceiling desperately needed to be painted. Apparently, the previous owners flung pancakes and let them splatter overhead. (Much like the speakeasy closet, we had decided to rewrite the kitchen's history with "pancakes" and not "meth lab residue.")

The dining room was now painted a hue called Lilting Laughter, an annoyingly vague name that really meant "warm neutral." (When working on that room, one of my best friends would let out a hysterical shriek and then yell "*Lilting!*") The fist-sized holes had been patched and baseboards had been secured, but other than that, the room was in stasis. We all agreed that painting over the ceiling and removing all evidence of the Jump On The Bed With A Marker game could wait a little longer. (Pro tip: paint all ceilings *before* moving in. See: Kitchen.) Right before the baby was born, I revisited this room. Since it had originally needed the least amount of work (that's right, even with markers on the ceiling, it was still the room that company saw first), I had let a lot of things slide. I finally spackled the smaller holes along the baseboard and attempted to fully remove all traces of those "no residue" adhesive squares. It eventually took multiple dampened cloths, a file, and copious amount of sanding to get those things off. I found myself wishing that my house had been constructed from those squares.

The first floor bath which, when we were still touring the joint, had the dubious honor of being the nicest room in the house, still possessed a new pedestal sink and newish looking toilet. It also boasted a peeling teal-colored ceiling. We painted it white. *Five times.* Which drove home, yet again, the necessity to paint before moving in. *Before*, people.

In the front of the house was the formal living room, which was deemed "formal" only because we clearly also had the space for a "casual" living room as well as a "business casual" one. (The construction of the house was iffy, but you sure as heck couldn't knock the square footage.) I had chosen the aforementioned Cajun Red for this room, which my excellent friends dutifully painted it, and I immediately fell even more in love with my choice.

My mother had warned me over and over that the color was going to be a mistake. It was too bright. Red? Choose a neutral. Because you have to *live* there. But as soon as she saw it, she loved it as well; it was that perfect a choice. (I once even overheard her- jokingly, she claims- taking credit for its hue.)

The color had been inspired from a deep shade in a painting gifted to us by P.J.'s parents; a lonely red caboose on a dusty path. (I'm totally emoting here; I have no idea whether or not the caboose was lonely. Maybe he just had buyer's remorse and was ruing his decision to no longer rent his train track.)

The painting signified P.J.'s place in his family as the "caboose" of five and it struck a chord with me not only because red is my favorite color, but also because the caboose was not the only one questioning his life's choices. I would recline on the hard-won couch (which now possessed both sections) and hide the cigarette burn with my legs while hoping that the rest of the house would someday look as nice as this one room. To have these lovely thoughts, I would need to be facing away from the rusted picture window and avert my eyes from the water-stained front door and hallway. But if I looked up at the wrought iron chandelier with its twisting vines and soft glow, it was a lot easier.

The small former master bedroom off of the living room

was eventually going to be my office. In preparation of the Great Works which would be penned in this room, it was painted a soft color called Muffin Mix. P.J. called it This Room Is *Also* Rather Pink, Please Do Not Put Any Future Son Of Mine In Here. I thought that was rather close-minded of him. (Also, why would I ever put a baby in a room with windows that had been blacked out by tempera paint?)

I had mixed feelings about the downstairs. For starters, you needed to get there via a staircase that had been painted and re-painted so many times that the texture could only be called "bumpy." The bottom of the stairs featured ancient vinyl tiles that no longer cared to be stuck to the floor and happily skidded around every time they were stepped upon.

The laundry room also featured independently minded vinyl tiles and our rather expensive collection of water-specific appliances: the most basic washer and dryer on the market, a skinny water heater, and the replacement boiler with copper tubing stuck on the side for annual bleeding of the pipes. (We were later informed that this was not a legitimate apparatus for a boiler to have. We were shocked. Shocked! Are you saying that a company who repeatedly stole radiator endcaps were perhaps also responsible for MacGyvering our heating system?)

The full bathroom at the bottom of the stairs was still a horror show of a room. Despite its multiple scrubbings, it never lost its dirty feel. Perhaps it was the smell that had intensified, the one that had recently led an exterminator to believe that a rat had died within its walls and was slowly rotting away. Which totally explained the late summer swarm of gigantic black horseflies. (Actual quote: "By the time the horseflies have arrived, the majority of the decay has actually taken place." We were comforted!) Regardless of its convenience to the lower level's rooms, I refused to use it. I would happily walk upstairs to pee, thanks all the same.

Remember how I had viewed the Summer Kitchen as an extravagant extra room? And how it soon became The Island Of Misfit Toys for our bed frame and storage? Despite its illegally installed picture window and even after the removal of the broken and putrid water-filled appliances from the room, it still wasn't quite as posh as I'd hoped. This may have been due entirely to the fact that P.J.'s best friend stored the eighty percent of his former apartment in that one room for a month. Then two. Then- oh, go ahead. We're not using it for anything besides growing mold in the walls. (Which is a great fifth grade science fair project, but a completely terrible endeavor for a homeowner.)

We were stuck with sky blue diamond-shaped ceramic tiles spanning all of the downstairs flooring. I imagine this would have been a really great design choice for a Miami hotel lobby circa 1971. Sadly, we did not own such a hotel. (Nor could we afford to leave the state for a goodly bit of the foreseeable future.) But, as it covered a decently working radiant heating system in the floors, it would have to stay for now. To combat this, we slathered cool tones atop the sickly pumpkin shade that had run amok on all of the lower level's walls. The makeshift curtain rod I had invented allowed for Ikea curtains to grace the picture windows and (kind of) hide the fact that the front lawn was ridiculously overgrown with weeds and scraggly rose bushes.

The lower level bedroom, which would double as P.J.'s office, was painted a grayer shade of blue. And that was it. There was nothing we could do about the flimsy mirrored closet doors, nor the speakeasy behind them. The chipped windowsills were hidden by tacky metal blinds that stayed tightly closed to ward off any Peeping Tomàs that might be in our walkway. But as long as we never needed to let any air/cigarette smoke into this room, it would make a nice place for company to sleep, we thought. And the Texas ghost bug was gone, too!

The designation of this room did, however, make us pose the question: Why did we feel the need to have so many damn "offices?" Were we CPAs?

The backyard was still a decently wide expanse of a dirt pile. Plastic strips segmented where a vegetable garden ought to be, where some bushes used to be, and where more dirt currently was. The cracked cement patio had a gargantuan stain of what I chose to believe was oil.

Our garage was a warehouse of doors, not the least of which was the one now attached to the opener. The others were propped against the garage walls; interior doors, exterior doors, hallway closet doors, bedroom doors that had been punched through, and at least one hollow door filled with spiders. But since the car now fit safely inside of the garage, we considered it a check in the "finished" category.

Same goes for the recently rinsed-out shed, even though I would never ever (in a million trillion years) check it out for myself.

Rooms in the house notwithstanding, I had a bizarre need to finish everything I had wanted to do in the history of ever. Remember the episode of *Full House* where Uncle Jesse needed to jump out of an airplane before he married Becky? It was kind of like that, except the tree in which I became entangled was actually a closet full of baby hangers.

Every library book needed to be returned. And then I'd go back and read the ones I didn't fully savor because, you know, *this was it for reading.*

All gift cards must be spent. What if I died and never got to redeem those fifty bucks towards Motherhood Maternity? Or that Taco Bell punch card? I did not want those to be my last conscious thoughts before being suffocated by my own labor headband. Or strapped to a table while P.J. told me how great I was doing.

The week before I checked into the hospital was spent cursing the parking situation in the greater Chicagoland area. The priority parking spots for pregnant women (those are real!)

in front of most baby stores were always full. I began to slowly circle the lots, waiting for their occupants to come out and affirm how pregnant they really were. I also wondered how certain stores would feel about my double-parking perpendicular to the automatic doors. Like, just halfway inside of them.

Walking had become something for which I demanded applause and recognition. (Take away my lung space and the feelings in my lower extremities and I get *awfully* whiny.)

My favorite errand was when I spent a gift certificate at a certain not-to-be-named overpriced Mommy Boutique. They had racks and racks of evening wear. Silk capris. Organic woven robes.

I tried on a hoodie.

In the dressing room, however, they possessed a simply magical and comically incredible apparatus called the Belly Sizer. This half melon attached to a Velcro belt served as a suggestion size for slender women wondering how to purchase third trimester apparel.

You could have fit three of them within the radius of my actual belly. One of them could have been substituted for my boob.

I laughed about this for a few moments. Then I teared up. After that, I left to go get some nachos.

Before this whole baby/house two-step, I had filled my weekends and nights with theatre. Some was stuff I had written, others were shows in which I performed, and still others were plays in which I performed but lied to my friends about (because they would hate it/I would hate myself). Being as one can only handle so much drama at a time- including actual staged drama- I took a bit of a break to cook the kid and hammer things to other things. But towards the end of my pregnancy, I was suddenly desperate to complete some new body of work, in case my own body was out of commission for a good fifteen years. Proving what, I'm not sure. That I was capable of work other than illegally hiring a contractor to replace a picture window before the home was "technically" ours? Maybe.

I was still blogging 24/7 about house and pregnancy adventures. The silver lining of all of my homeowner and gastrointestinal fiascos was that I'd never had more to write about, and I'd also found some sweet niches on the internet for which some folks were willing to pay extremely paltry amounts. This wasn't *theatre*, though. Where was the mounting tension? The crew of over-caffeinated people in stage blacks moaning about exhaustion? And there were literally zero people applauding in front of me. (A phenomenon that has occurred even during some of my plays, but I digress.) Blogging is good for a lot of things like instant gratification and free mugs, but terrible for physical storytelling and applause.

However, my playwriting attempts had seemed to stall out even when I did try to have something staged. This could be blamed on the fact that I now possessed a complete inability to *not* write about pregnancy. It was, quite literally, the only dialogue that would appear on the page. Abandoned single mothers. Hilarious pregnancy dreams. Cautionary tales of husbands who wouldn't make a midnight run for Italian ice. Compelling stuff, all, but rather specifically marketed.

Since my biological clock was on overdrive- and had been for the past year- part of me naturally assumed that all women could relate to the Baby Blinders that I had been wearing. This was not necessarily the case.

After the curtain went down on my last one-act concerning an accidental pregnancy and a girl being berated by her childhood teddy bear (actual plot line), I decided to let the theatre thing hang until the kid came along. And I could write normally again.

Whatever that meant.

Mentally, I was freeing myself up. Physically, I was booked. In fact, I was downright swamped by the task of imploding from the chest cavity downwards.

I began to get terrifyingly epic hiccups. Since the kiddo was also hiccupping non-stop, I worried for the turbulent space station in which he or she resided. Also, on a slightly lesser note, I feared I might pop a lung. And my bladder, never the most stalwart of my organs, threatened to just give out on me. Regardless of the number of Kegel exercises I would (pretend to) do in a day. I'm pretty sure I know why those didn't work, though: Because even writing about it makes me feel creepy.

P.J. and I entered into a period which we lovingly termed The Time When We Didn't Even *Know* What We Should Be Fearing. I decided that P.J. and I should embark on Date Night Month. We really didn't have the money. Or the time. Not to mention the energy. But- and this is embarrassing- I had started to heed the Just Waits and fully believed that nothing would ever be the same.

And of course it wouldn't. But that didn't necessitate dining out each night. (If I could do it over again, I would've slept.) But Date at Night we did. And let's just put it out there that 24 year-old Keely would be appalled by 29 year-old Keely's idea of a Good Date.

We saw *Where The Wild Things Are* in the theater and (I) wept at the joyous thought of my future (gender non-specific) son. Sure, I had to take two pee breaks and we quite possibly purchased more popcorn than could have fed our future fully realized family, but we were Out And About.

Then there was the day that we hiked a trail at the nearby forest preserve and spied a Mama and baby deer nesting together. I wept at that sight, too, which seemed to be a common occurrence and no longer needed acknowledgment from P.J. or anyone who happened to be around me.

Further down the path we saw a gigantic buck and P.J. informed him that his family was still fine and undisturbed. I think they had a moment of male understanding.

All of that fresh air and well-being made us hungry, so we stopped at a Drive-Thru diner which boasted the most impressive malt and milkshake menu we'd ever seen, not to mention bags of the greasiest and easily most satisfying fries one could purchase. We still considered that day a check in the Exercise column.

Then there was the mad dash to use up gift certificates and birthday presents, including a cooking class that I had given to P.J. for his birthday four years prior. There's nothing like cooking lobster thermidor in a boiling hot room with a staff eyeing your bottom (questioning the elasticity of pants/checking to see if one's water had broken) to remind you of how much fun you're having. That said, we ate really well. And I got the much-coveted counter space with a stool, ha *ha*.

We ate at Irish pubs and French bistros. Got two-for-one ice cream cones. (To share, if you must know. Not just for *me*.) Had high tea at the Drake Hotel and pretended we were awesome enough to be allowed inside. (It worked. Once.)

There was also the attempt to see every piece of staged theatre in which our friends were currently working. Quite simply, if this was the end of Life As We Know It/If I Die On The Operating Table, our friends would have no reason to doubt the sincerity of our affection. Which no true friend really would think if I died in childbirth, anyhow. But late-term pregnancy logic and gentle actions were not my friends. My friends with social lives were my friends.

At least they couldn't deny my appearance at events. I was pretty hard to miss.

CHAPTER TEN

(Oh boy…)

The morning of my kid's birth was spent like any other Thursday. Except for the fact that I was cleaning like a speed freak (do they clean?), trying *not* to think about what a C-section entailed, and packing and re-packing an L.L. Bean bag within an inch of its life, it was really like any other day.

I got up at the crack of dawn to make myself breakfast. No food past 6:30am, per hospital's orders? *You got it.*

I blogged about how calm yet excited I was. Really. Calm n' excited. Just a normal day. And *man* if you couldn't eat off of my kitchen floors. I mean, *I* couldn't because of the upcoming surgery, but any other visiting crazy person could.

P.J. decided to work from home that morning. Bless him. We'd both had this hilarious notion that we'd go about our mornings productively and, at the appropriate time, calmly drive over to the hospital and simply have a child. No need to amend the day's activities in the slightest.

And except for the fact that we couldn't keep a single thought in our heads at all, I think we succeeded rather nicely.

We were as ready as we could possibly be to have this child. Which means: exactly nothing. Because even in our advanced stage of Mental Readiness, we were still Not Ready. You know how newlyweds say they're not ready to have a child when pressured by meddling relatives? And people say "Oh, you'll *never* be ready. If people waited 'til they were *ready*, there'd be no children in the world!" Turns out, that's true. Because even after being Not Ready for this baby's existence and spending close to nine months being Not Ready to give birth, we were still wholly Not Ready on the kid's purported birthday. It wasn't that we were having doubts about the kid. Everything else in our lives up to this point, sure, but not the kid. We already loved this baby. We just wished we could plan (and over-plan) for another nine months or so. Like an elephant.

We ended up heading to the hospital a little earlier than planned, probably due to the fact that I was hovering around the passenger seat and P.J. felt sorry for me. So off we drove to have our boy. Even though we were still clueless as to the actual gender of this kid, we had long ago given up any pretense of gender non-specifics. "Him" it was.

As we enjoyed our quiet drive on that sunny October day, we actually laughed to ourselves about how it would be such a hoot if our son was actually a daughter!

Those thoughts were quickly put out of our minds as we turned our attention to important things like finding the perfect song on the radio and idly complaining about the darned traffic. We were also deliciously weirded out by the temporarily vacant car seat right behind us.

We arrived at the hospital well before our mandatory arrival time of noon (it was maybe 11am, tops), and had the door held open for us by a valet guy. (No kidding. Prentice Hospital is a *lot* like The Four Seasons.)

"Happy birthday, Mom," he cheerfully told me.

This caused me to cry. P.J. apologized for me and we went inside.

After we checked in and they determined that I was indeed extremely pregnant and all of my info matched up with all of their info, they informed us that we could head up to Labor and Delivery. Oh boy! *Now* we'd have a baby!

Except for the fact that they really weren't ready for us at all.

Apparently, emergency C-sections take crazy precedence over those regular ol' planned ones. And there were three of them that afternoon. (Come *on*!) Even this would have been okay if not for the pack of Nervous Nellies seated with us in the waiting room and anticipating news of their own impending grandkids, nieces and nephews.

That's right; we sat in the waiting room for two hours with the non-pregnant riff raff.

All the while, we had to try really hard to not hear about everything that had *gone* wrong, *could* go wrong, and were *probably* going wrong at this very instant in the operating rooms for all three women.

It was difficult to focus on my Sudoku.

Finally, they called my name and led me to a prep space that would double as my recovery room. And man, did they make up for lost time! Two nurses poked, prodded, and I.V.'d me up while a third verified my info yet again. (I guess they really wanted to make sure I was pregnant.) They took some blood. They took more blood for the umbilical cord donation kit, an endeavor about which I had previously been feeling Altruistic and Good, but which now I was rethinking, as I dearly wanted people to just stop touching me.

P.J., for his part, did his best to nod seriously at any information received. He was also prepping and double-checking the blank "It's A…" email we had set up with family and friends' contacts for the ease of communication once we knew what "It" was.

All too soon it was time for me to make the long walk to the O.R. And that had to be done alone. I had been dreading the solo act of the spinal; well, *solo* unless you count the anesthesiologist, my O.B., and the team of nurses who had to be present as well. But other than them, it was the long march of solitude.

It had been built up in my mind as this terrifying ritual of torture, and something to endure while the weak-stomached Dads paced in the hall. This is not a[n overly] sexist remark.

The Great Expectations nurse told a story about a father-to-be who passed out at the sight of the mammoth epidural needle... and dragged his wife off of the table as he fell. *Not Cool.*

That said, I would have liked a bit more moral support in my time of fright than Samuel, my Beanie Baby duck whom I clutched in my hands.

Correct. I walked in to have my first child while carrying a small stuffed animal. I don't feel too much shame over this, as he had been present for every major surgery since the age of twelve. He knows the drill.

So. The spinal.

A really nice guy named Mike introduced himself as my anesthesiologist and made some mandatory joke about this being his first day. Ha *ha*. (Does everyone make this joke? It needs to stop.) Anyway, I think his name was Mike. It may not have been. I was a little too busy hyperventilating in fear to play Name Pneumonics. (My name is *Mike* and I live in *Manhattan* and I like *Marmalade*. No time for those shenanigans.)

Perhaps his small talk was intended to distract me from the knowledge that a) he was taping some sort of cat's cradle pattern on my back in preparation for the big ol' needle or b) my naked butt was now on display to the room at large, but he needn't have worried. Tape did not bother me. Nor, at this point in the pregnancy, did public nudity.

While this prep was going on, my actual doctor entered the room and made a shocking discovery: this was not a latex free operating room.

It wasn't enough that I was allergic to the chili pepper. Special enough as I was, I've also had a latex sensitivity since the age of ten. Every time I had left the orthodontist's office, it looked like I had gotten shot up with Botox. Not only was it rare to see a Botoxed tween back in those days, it was even rarer to hear of a latex allergy back in 1990. The young menfolk of Pittsfield, Massachusetts had had a field day with that little bit of info. Go on, make your quip. I've heard it before. (Through my tears in the girls' bathroom stall.)

But yes, very allergic. So I watched as trays and trays of utensils were rolled out and back into the room, adding a good fifteen minutes of completely panicked existence to my surgery.

Finally, it was time to begin. My doctor announced his name, the date, and the type of surgery. I thought it was a game and announced my name as well. I even acknowledged the duck.

This really happened.

Since he had, in fact, been recording the info for audio posterity, we had to start again. But, truly, I really was past any point of embarrassment. I think everyone in the room was well-equipped to deal with my nervous energies and subsequent weirdness.

It was finally time for the needles. I had as close to an out-of-body experience as I've ever had (even surpassing the pee-covered stick moment), thinking about *how I'd been dreading this one single moment for months and months and finally it was here.* (Yes, the same could be said about the anticipation of the whole "having a child" thing too, but this was my darkest moment.) Remembering a bit of helpful info someone had told me early on in the pregnancy, I hunched my back hard into a Pilates curl. Apparently this makes it easier to get the shots in the right places and takes away some of the pinching.

This made me extra glad I had been attempting to "work out" so much during the first parts of the pregnancy. *What if I hadn't known what a Pilates curl was?* Pinch City.

To tell the truth, I barely felt the first numbing shot. Less so for the second. And when Mike announced that he was putting in the spinal, I realized that the talking about it was the worst part. Sure, it didn't feel awesome, but it was more of a weird, nervy pressure and an instantaneous cold.

I was so proud of myself for not vomiting in fear, but my work wasn't yet done. Apparently, I was quickly on my way to becoming a dead weight, so I "helped" the nurses swing my legs up and around to the table. Things sped up from there. A tent was quickly erected. I half-felt through my lower extremities that someone was attempting to catheterize me and I actually let out a token protest. (Oh, *that's* too invasive? *Now* we're setting boundaries?)

I was then strapped down onto the table. Just like in the videos! I was informed that some women didn't care for this initial part of lying down, as it immobilized their chests and made them feel like they couldn't breathe. I informed anyone who would listen that I hadn't been able to use my lungs since month five, since The Bitsy had a tendency towards jungle gym-like ribcage activity.) I dug the numbness. Also, resting.

At one point I got really woozy but before I could even utter a word, Mike reassured me that he was on it. I *loved* Mike. Again, I'm not sure if this was his actual name or the drug-induced one I created for him. Regardless, I was ready to name my kid after him.

Finally, after what seemed like a year, a scrubbed-up P.J. was seated beside my head. He kissed me. I was so relieved to see him that I almost cried. Despite this, I lashed out in a delightfully panicked sort of way that P.J. was (sadly) more than used to.

And I'm pretty sure I told him that I was never going home with him again.

The nurses laughed and so I began to regale them with stories of how he and I met, and how neither one of us ever expected the relationship to go anywhere. (I love a captive audience.) I added that we had basically only agreed to go out for a drink.

A nurse wondered aloud what was in that drink. It was a fair question.

The prep work on the end of the surgical staff took a few more minutes. My wandering mind began to panic about what, exactly, they were doing to me. And, since I had (unfortunately) seen the videos, I knew. A lot.

So I begged P.J. to tell me stories about old shows we had performed together (like the one where he played a tongue-less hick and I was a tree who had to hit him with a branch), that time we had snorkeled on our honeymoon and he was chased by a smallish barracuda, anecdotes about the cats being all catlike, *anything*. P.J. took a deep breath, disregarded the imminent questioning of his manhood, and embellished all of my favorite stories.

When he got to the part of our wedding prep where we had watched *Far And Away* as a five part miniseries, I kinda felt for P.J., because Mike was definitely wondering what this guy's deal was. But I'm sure P.J. and I both agreed that it was a small price to pay for my momentary mental relief.

The doctor then announced that he was making the first incision. Even though it was for the benefit of the audio recorder, I immediately wished that he hadn't shared. Because, what, did I have veto power? Was I supposed to tell him how much it hurt? I braced myself to feel…something, I suppose. Gloriously, I did not.

Seventeen minutes later he announced that I should feel a considerable relief in pressure. For the baby was *just about* out. My first thought was, "Oh my God, the space in my upper chest cavity feels so *good!*"

Then I wondered about the baby.

Then I wondered about the rapid fire speed in which the

kid was removed. Was someone *chasing us?*

P.J. was eager to see his child and had almost looked over the curtain once or twice. He was batted back for his own good. No one needs to see his wife filleted like a sea bass. Finally, the doctor asked P.J. if he wanted to let me know what we had.

P.J. jumped up and peered over. There was nothing but silence. P.J. later told me that he was slightly confused and had been looking awfully hard for something. In its absence, he realized exactly what kind of kid we'd be taking home with us.

"It's…a *girl!*"

He laughed. I laughed. The nurses laughed, too, but I'm pretty sure they also wondered why, exactly, that was quite so funny.

The boy I had had multiple dreams about, the child who had been pawed by strangers in my tummy and proclaimed to be a son, turned out to be none other than our daughter.

And the monstrous size I had feared as well as the gargantuan feet that had kicked me repeatedly throughout the months? A whopping 6lbs, 15oz., and 19 inches long. A baby ladybug.

I'll admit it, my initial shock colored my first thoughts. I wasn't disappointed- not by any stretch- but the DuraMorph was making my response times a little laggy. It wasn't until I saw my daughter getting weighed and measured across the room that my thoughts of "Oh look, someone had a baby girl" turned to "*And it's us!*"

There was more laughter on my part. I'm certain at least one nurse contemplated calling Child Services.

And then there she was beside me, curled up in P.J.'s arms. Little bow lips, a furrowed brow, and concerned eyes. Between blinks (hers *and* mine) I could see that the color was an indeterminate bluish grey which threatened to turn brown at any second. And the curls peeking out from under her cap were either or brown or gold or a combination of both. So, yes. I really had no idea what my own child looked like. It didn't matter what her features were doing. She was easily the most gorgeous thing that either of us had ever witnessed.

And if I live to be a thousand and two, I will *never* forget that first brush of my lips and nose against her head. (I was still strapped in, if you'll recall. Again, just like on the video!) The scent of her New Baby Skin (*much* better than New Car Smell) and feel of her scrunchy pink hat against my cheek are forever etched into my mind as the nicest things I'd ever experienced.

"Hey there, Nora Jane."

Baby Nora looked confused. And tired. Slightly ticked. But still ridiculously cute. I glanced over at P.J. and decided then and there that I really liked him. And I'm pretty sure he was thinking the exact same thing about me.

Less than an hour later, they wheeled me out of the O.R. and I clutched my newborn kiddo in my recently freed arms. Maybe it was the endorphins, or perhaps the extra shot of morphine they pumped into me on the way out, but I couldn't recall a time when I had ever been more contented.

I had a slightly odd moment's thought of wondering how- exactly- had all of this happened? I mean, I *knew*. (There was wine involved.) But the exact details of getting from Point A (and all of its nebulous verbs) to Point B (and its rather concrete nouns) were a blurry whirlwind. As I stared and re-focused my eyes at this chubby-cheeked, squinty little bundle of velvet, that suddenly seemed like an okay way to jive.

I had a brief Mompiphany. I had a fleeting moment where I realized not every single thing in my new life as a parent would be easily charted out or would fall into place. It was so strong that it almost rolled over into Homeownerpiphany Land.

"Shh," my rational side assured me. "Don't worry about plans and schemes and How Things Ought To Go. This is life. And it's awesome. Roll with it."

This unexpectedly pleasant notion calmed me. Right until the morphine steamrolled me back into twilight, shoving all coherent thought into the attic of my brain for the next four months.

Even when Nora Jane was only an hour old, I had already decided that I liked being her Mom. Aside from that whole Growing Her And Letting Them Tug Her Out Of Me thing, I had literally done nothing motherly for her as yet. There was time for that, I was sure. I felt like a grownup. One with a kid and a half-realized house and a guy at my side who had just become a Dad.

I informed P.J. that I wanted eight more kids. As soon as possible. He laughed, then wondered if it was safe to laugh, then decided it was as I was still heavily medicated, then debated if there was anything in our vows that would prevent him from smothering my face with the hospital-issued plastic pillow.

CHAPTER ELEVEN

(Oh, girl.)

The rest of the hospital stay was a whirlwind. Maybe a drug-wind. I had made exceptional friends with that previously mentioned substance called DuraMorph. (Morphine for the duration! Clever.) It made the first twenty four hours absolute bliss, if you're into that whole Feeling Nothing thing. Which I most definitely was. Even seeing the metal staples on my abdomen was enough reality for me.

People came and went, patted Nora, patted me, told me how pretty she was (true), how great I looked (untrue), and I got to eat real food. Quite possibly sooner than was recommended. But I was starving. I do not fast well. Pancakes and a side salad at 7pm? That'll do.

That evening was rather sublime. The three of us snuggled in for our first night as a family. Nora was swaddled on my chest, I was swaddled (in various easily opened/not so easily secured pieces of hospital couture) on my bed, and P.J. pretended to be just fine on a skinny pull-out couch.

He played lullaby versions of The Beatles and a mellow bluegrass mix. Nora really seemed to like both, proving that she was already a connoisseur of good tunes. We were both blown away by her early aptitude for music and her easygoing nature. (The DuraMorph had *nothing* to do with it. She was making the choice to be lulled.)

My mother flew into Chicago early the next morning and came straight to the hospital. I would have been unaware of her entrance if not for the fact that she had somehow timed her arrival to a few minutes after the doctor came to check my incision. During my exam, we heard the door open from behind the curtain, which had been pulled closed around the rod. Then we heard nothing. Then we heard the unmistakable sound of someone attempting to muffle sniffling.

My doctor looked alarmed. I wasn't. (I come from a long line of happy criers.)

"Mom?"

"Hi honey." (Sniffle.)

"Want to come actually *see* the baby?"

"Yes. Just give me a minute." (Sniffle.)

The doctor stared questioningly at me. I nodded comfortingly. There was no need to alert the staff; everything was completely normal. My mother proceeded to cry at us from behind the curtain for the next few minutes, eventually working up to crying at us from the foot of the bed.

The timing of my mother's entrance with my doctor's exam also allowed my Mom to question the doctor about my C-section, the incision, and my future childbearing practices. This I highly recommend. After all, the doctor might be a "professional," but he's not a "mom," and he's certainly not My

Mom. Thus, until certain things are asked and answered (fully), they're not exactly valid or safe. That's all I'm saying.

She also happened to be present when a woman from the nearby church visited to say a little blessing for the baby. I was touched, as I was thoroughly enjoying each time anyone acknowledged that there was a new baby (and she was mine). My mother was less sure of any newcomers. And when the woman sneezed into her hand (as opposed to the trendy crook of the arm)? My mother widened her eyes and Stared. The. Woman. Down. Pursed her lips. Made significant facial gestures. And smiled politely until the woman left.

"That's nice," she said as she looked at the potentially germy and baby-endangering wooden keepsake cross. Even though it was obviously *not* nice, not nice at all.

My mother was of the opinion that people (even people *of the church*) should not be allowed to hold, see, or give things to this *unbelievably wonderful and brand-new child* without at least three forms of I.D. and a military physical.

I totally agreed with her but, as previously mentioned, the meds were dulling such things as Mama Bear instincts. Besides- a wooden keepsake cross!

Prentice Hospital is a nice place to have a kid. Even the food is awesome. So good, in fact, that when I asked a nurse what my meal allowance was and she told me that I got three meals and two snacks, *I thought she meant for the whole stay.*

That first day I ate like a bird to make it last. I made a snack into dinner- which I shared with my husband. When my mother (kindly) called out the utter insanity of my thought process, I realized that, yes, making a post-operative new mother nibble on snack sized portions *would* be rather cruel and unhealthy.

I soon made up for the error of my ways, as evidenced by the paper trail. The receipts for each order listed out things like carbohydrates, protein, and calories. This is a terrible practice and needs to be discontinued immediately. If I want to eat two pieces of meatloaf and follow it up with more than my fair share of bread pudding (and some corn and some potatoes and a salad with Jell-o on top of it), I *really* don't need anyone telling me that my dinner racked up two thousand calories.

Even with the great meal service, I had been dreaming of sushi since Day 2 of my pregnancy. P.J. was a gem and treated me to my beloved spicy tuna rolls and Hamachi for the next evening's dinner. (I also missed red wine, but he told me not to push it.) Everyone who heard about our sushi plan thought that it was a terrible idea for the relative instability of my post-operative, still-on-morphine belly. But guess what? Great sushi is *never* a poor decision.

As long as one isn't pregnant, trying to save money, or allergic to fish. Then- avoid.

Sadly, that night marked the end of my brief affair with

DuraMorph. My ol' pal Blinding Pain came to spend the night. With it, came a bizarre abdominal rash that was an allergic reaction to the iodine used in the surgery. Or maybe it was the medical tape. Perhaps even the morphine itself. So they slathered me with hydrocortisone cream and rationed my meds to once every four hours for the hard stuff, and every six hours for the weak stuff. ·

I was in a ridiculous amount of pain, but now I was also sticking to my sheets and slimy from the cream. This made me crabby. (We'll go with "crabby.")

Luckily, I had a sweet-faced 2am buddy who was content to ogle my face and let me kiss hers. Snuggle endorphins are a very real thing. (Of course, I'm referring to Nora. P.J. was otherwise occupied with trying to shove the couch into some semblance of a comfy bed.)

Still, issues with various gastrointestinal things led me to ask a nurse for some Gas-X pills. Trapped post-op gas? Questionable amounts of sushi on an unprepared stomach? Jury's still out. But right before I took the pills, I had the moronic moment of asking if they were "safe for the baby" whom I was nursing. (I felt like the idiotic woman in the epidural video who asked if the needle would hurt.)

The nurse paused. Looked at me. Stared pointedly at my multiple I.V.s and cups holding future doses of Hydrocodone.

She told me that *now* was not the time to start worrying about drugs.

So I didn't.

(Sorry, Nora.)

Our day nurse had been a soothing angel of a woman. She was so *proud* of me for holding Nora in the right nursing position, wasn't I *wonderful* to be drinking all of the water she had placed in the Slurpee-sized bucket, and wasn't Nora just the *prettiest* name? I loved this nurse.

The night nurse had no time for these things. She was the one who had removed my constant stream of morphine and yanked out the catheter. (Granted, both of these things were inevitably going to happen, but I felt good blaming my unhappiness on one brusque person.) She made me walk to the bathroom and pee. And, she told me, she wanted to see me walk a lap around the maternity hall. I reminded her that I had just had a C-section. She nodded like this was news, like I was her first post-op new mother.

"Get up."

It hurt. There was blood. I felt (and looked) like I had been hit by a truck twice. Holding my puffy and bruised incision with one hand (and trying to hide the fact that I was wearing mesh underwear with the other), I demanded that P.J. not look. He calmly told me that he had seen worse. (This did not make me feel better. You've seen *worse*? Where, on the side of the road? In snuff films?)

The night nurse also demanded that I nurse the baby more. Like, wake her up (wake her *up!?*) and feed her every two hours. At least.

A nanny would have had no way of knowing what experienced mothers know all too well; the night shift nurses are supposed to scare first-time Moms. They just are. Because breast milk doesn't immediately appear once the baby does. (Besides the occasional- and terrifying- quick spurts of third trimester lactation. That would sustain nothing and no one, excepting perhaps the plot for a freaky short story.) However, since the baby does indeed nurse immediately if being breastfed, the kiddo generally loses a crazy amount of weight during the hospital stay due to the lack of actual food coming from the breasts. This is normal.

But, adding to what I didn't know was that a ten percent weight loss from the child's birth weight would require this nurse to berate me into just trying to "feed her again." She followed this up with a warning that Nora would be whisked off to the nursery for the evening if her "numbers" didn't improve.

And they'd have to give her formula. At the time, this was my worst motherly fear. (For I was an ignorant New Mother With Ideas. There is *so* much stuff to fear, fear not! Or fear on!)

And if that didn't work, they'd start her on an I.V., as she was looking "a little dehydrated." (See? Worse!)

This freak out fest occurred on the second night, the time after any surgery when body pain can be likened to a scale of 1 to a gazillion (as opposed to the prior day's paltry 1 to 10). And it coincided with the fluctuating hormones so common to postpartum women. (It also cannot be mentioned enough that the DuraMorph train had left the station.)

P.J. was also absent for a portion of this evening, leaving me to believe that I was independently starving my child and potentially the worst parent ever.

There were tears.

Then there were more tears when P.J. returned and suggested that perhaps an hour of rest while Nora visited the nursery would be best for everyone. He (nicely) pointed out that I hadn't slept for more than ten minutes in the past forty eight hours. I (not so nicely) asked him why he hated me and our baby. And I wondered why he wanted Nora to feel abandoned and bereft. And starving. She was *starving*.

Again, I'm no medical professional, but I'm pretty sure that none of those factors and events (and certainly none of them together) leads to a relaxed mother with a newfound ability to fill her boobs. Could be wrong, though.

By the end of that evening, we had all come to some sort of understanding. The nurse eased the heck up (and stopped shaking her head while writing numbers on my dry erase board like a disappointed Russian judge), P.J. stopped trying to steal my baby, and I was able to rest, safe in the knowledge that Nora was comfy (but *starving*) in her hospital bassinet at the foot of my bed. Occasionally, Nora would let out a mouse-like squeak and turn her head from side to side. We'd lock eyes and I'd miss her so fiercely that I would demand that P.J. bring her to me immediately. He would sleepily point out that maybe she *wasn't* locking eyes with me, as he was fairly certain that her eyes couldn't yet focus that far.

I would politely inform him that, since he had not yet (to the best of my abilities) carried a child *inside of him*, he wouldn't quite understand how painful it was to be even three feet apart from his baby for the first time ever.

He agreed. Then he begged me to go to sleep. So I did. (With one eye open in case he had more thoughts about that hospital-issued pillow.)

Maybe it wasn't the most healing of rests, though. P.J. might have looked asleep, but I wasn't going to risk it. Nora was *not* going to the nursery, and I was *not* going to be smothered in my sleep.

Besides, I wanted to be awake for when my boobs were ready to nurse someone.

Multiple friends visited during my hospital stay (and braved my mother's sporadic Stern Eye). We were bombarded with voicemails, emails, and a barrage of Facebook posts. I was consoled for needing to have a C-section. (Was I sad that I didn't really get to "have" Nora? Note: Never say this to anyone, ever. If the postpartum parent in question is truly a loving, responsible, and intelligent human being, they won't have cared if the kid was yanked from their nostril so long as everyone involved is now healthy.) I was also congratulated for *getting* to have a C-section. (No laboring! What a treat.)

One of the things I apparently narrowly avoided was (to the best of my knowledge) pooping on the delivery room table. A lot of people were and are deeply concerned about this. Something about the idea of being naked, vulnerable, and in pain, and you're going to add an embarrassingly gross bodily function into the mix? (Well, a bodily function that wasn't part of the initial deal, that is.) I get it, I do.

But here's my take on that; unless you're delivering at a strange, foreign hospital (and why are you traveling past 36 weeks of gestation?), every single person involved in your current scenario is either a) the medical staff who has seen not only *your* innards, but also the innards and outtards of a boggling number of people or b), the person responsible for your condition. And in that last case, seeing your poop should be the least bothersome thing running through *their* minds, preceded by how intensely wonderful you are for currently having their child, and quietly thanking God that it's not *them* up there wearing a fierce Labor Headband.

That said, when dealing with postpartum constipation, you really won't care *where* or in front of *whom* you go, as long as it finally just starts happening again. But if I keep up with talk like that, I really won't have to worry about postpartum birth control.

We are a long, long way from wearing eyeliner to bed and brushing our teeth right before dawn to impress the other party with our beauty and shockingly fresh breath.

The end of our hospital stay was marked by an event so spectacularly out of character that it managed to eke through my Hydrocodone haze and demand acknowledgement.

My husband, he of the Defensively Offensive Left Lane-Zooming Highway Driving, the one who views backups and construction as personal affronts to his path, chauffeured home his newborn daughter in the right-hand lane. Slowly. At least five miles per hour slower than the speed limit, and at least twenty miles per hour slower than I'd ever witnessed.

When I jokingly called him out on this, he informed me that he now had precious cargo riding along with him. (As opposed to whom and when prior to this, exactly?)

I decided to let that one go and bask in the bliss of our shared parenthood. There was plenty of time, after all.

The drive took nearly half an hour.

CHAPTER TWELVE

(*Homecoming.*)

Now that all of the hard work was done, I figured we'd be on Easy Street. After all, hadn't we grown a kid, found a home, (kinda) fixed a home, and produced said kid? And it definitely *was* easy, at least for the first three and a half weeks of live-in help. My parents, P.J.'s parents, and my oldest sister all came to assist out with housework, exceptional meals, and the best Nora-holding this side of anywhere.

It was exceptionally cool to have all of these additional hands.

It was exceptionally kind to have people (who took time off from their own lives) to wait on us hand and foot.

And it was exceptionally bizarre to have, for the first time since I was eight, someone coddle me and bring me anything I could possibly need. And even if I *didn't* need, but my mother felt that I *did* need. Like yogurt shakes (To help your milk come in!) and a blanket (Take a nap!) and the removal of said blanket (You're making me too hot, aren't you hot?) all day long.

Also strange was apologizing for how the kitchen was set up, the funky shower dial in the downstairs bath, and the occasional 2am siren. I had never realized how truly unlivable my house was until we were hosting family. I mean, sure, I could deal with things caving in and nauseating smells, but seeing houseguests deal with a jammed closet door? A real eye-opener.

And any time you have a mother staying at your home, the kitchen suddenly belongs to the Alpha Mother. Meaning, the spices will go where they ought to go. Sometimes this means on the counter. Other times it means they are thrown out and the correct kind are purchased. Things are placed in bowls- for later. Dish rags (not sponges) are utilized. And forget trying to find something on your own. Because *why aren't you resting?*

It was a huge adjustment for someone who was accustomed to having had things Just So for the better part of a decade- and cohabitating with a guy who was totally cool with this arrangement of things. The combination of meds, the pain, and sleepiness from dates with my middle-of-the-night newborn pal made me a touch whiny at times. Stir crazy at others.

That said, there are few scenarios in the world nicer than being tucked in for a nap, a soft newborn sleeping against your chest, and sleeping *until you feel like waking*, only to find your favorite kind of sandwich (egg salad mixed with tuna) waiting for you with a glass of your favorite beverage (vodka tonic- okay fine, lime seltzer) on the coffee table.

I didn't wash a single load of Nora's laundry until she had grown into the next size.

But eventually, people had to return to their lives, their jobs, their other children, and I had to learn to do this thing by myself.

I did have moments in the following weeks, however, when I wondered where my sous chefs had gone. Had she taken my laundry lady, too? And when the baby cried during my nap, *I* was expected to fetch her? The dinner thing also threw me for a loop. We had to have it every night? Even though we now had a baby with no concept of schedules or polite conversation?

In the darkest of these hours I'd get a text from my Mom, reminding me of the stew in the freezer. Or my mother-in-law would send cookies and encouraging notes. These were nice reminders that I had been a total brat during the blissful span of time where I got to have a baby and *be* a baby.

Aside from the first two nights post-op, healing from the C-section wasn't the horror show of which the Just Waits had warned me. Even with from the limitations of not lifting anything heavier than Nora, I felt pretty good. That is, except for those days when I couldn't deal with the clutter and way overdid the juggling of an infant and the attempt to run a downright Donna Reed household. On those days, I'd end up in extreme pain and overwhelmed by all the stuff I hadn't done. I'd compensate by refusing to do anything except snuggle with Nora for the next two days. This, of course, would only result in home squalor, forcing me to repeat the whole process. I'm not entirely sure why I felt so driven to have an orderly life during this time; after all, a newborn pretty much equates disorder. Physically and mentally, I was cluttered. Maybe it was the fact that I had never resided in this home without spending every waking hour trying to turn it into an actual abode. Perhaps it was because I had forgotten how to relax. Either way, it wasn't pretty. (Neither was I, but even in my frantic need for order, I decided it was totally cool to let myself go for a bit.)

After wallowing in my imagined failure for a hazy, indeterminate amount of time, I decided that I'd just focus on Nora. The rest could wait. In fact, I thought that this would be cinchy, due to my aforementioned nanny hubris. But regardless of my knowledge of all things baby, toddler, and kid, Nora found ways to freak the bejesus out of me. She innately knew all of my tricks and how to change the game. In short, she was the ultimate inside man, delivering a comeuppance of epic proportions.

Thinking that I could figure out this kid because of another kid's habits and dislikes (or nine other kids' habits and dislikes) was like thinking that a marathon of *Law & Order* episodes would help one pass a class concerning the Supreme Court. (Which one of us may or may not have done.)

I knew how to burp, hold, and soothe a baby, and I'd dealt with more than one colicky infant. But what about when my own newborn had belly issues and would spit up a projectile the distance from the couch to the coffee table? I was sure she was dying. (My oldest sister convinced me via phone that this was most likely not so.)

Nora's hair fell out in odd patches, horrifying me to no end. I mean, sure, other babies' hair fell out all the time, but I wanted expert opinion and documentation that this wasn't a brain disorder. (On Nora's part, not mine.) And no one- and no amount of web reading- could convince me that her hair would grow in before her junior prom. So I cried.

I discovered that a baby's hair falls out because all of their follicles grow at exactly the same time in the womb. Each strand has exactly the same life cycle, and at no other time in our lives does this naturally happen! I was fascinated by this bit of science. Freaked out, but fascinated.

I started to give Nora whimsical nicknames to combat my discomfort at her shiny pate. Ed Asner and I were just fine after that.

Although there was a brief period of time where I contemplated purchasing one of those spray-on hair color kits, like from those early '90s infomercials. I would've happily chosen that reddish-orange color for her, because that's the one I recall looking the coolest.

Then there was the time I almost ripped off her toe during a routine pajama change. (That's right, people- *I have been left alone with children for pay.*)

I stripped her down to find that one of her footly digits was getting rather purple and swollen. I couldn't figure out why this was happening, short of a life-threatening allergy or a skin plague. I eventually realized that a thin little hair (most likely mine, since all of hers had left us) was wrapped nine times to Tuesday around her middle toe. After a positively embarrassing amount of panicky inaction, I decided to just remove the thing. (The hair, not the toe. At least that was my hope going in.)

I went through a battery of ineffectively large tools; scissors, fingernails, and my teeth, to name a few. Finally I hit upon the perfect device. Nora's miniature nail clippers, those of the So Dangerous To Her Person That As Have Yet To Be Used variety were the perfect size for trimming a hair and salvaging a foot. And after a few terrifying and scarring moments (for both my psyche and the skin on the underside of her toe), her foot was released from its hairy prison. And she only had a minimum of blood on her foot to show for it. Ever try to bandage a toe smaller than the actual bandage? It's a fine study in proportions.

I also blamed myself for ruining her shiny new digestive tract. Despite my best intentions to keep her bedding, clothing, and toys as cat-free as possible, Nora would occasionally have a poop that contained tiny hairballs. Further proof of my Bad Mommyhood *or* conclusive evidence that she is actually part kitten? You be the judge.

She created diapers so epic that they demanded their own nomenclature. Sure, I'd changed disgustingly crazy diapers in the past decade, but had never experienced the volume of her up-the-back poosplosion. It soon became my kid's signature move. Running late for a doctor's appointment? Lemme just shoot some poop clear up to my neck for you. Or, I bet you *love* this pretty white sweater. You know what would look beautiful with it? Some liquid feces threatening to spill from the armholes.

We were both frightened and impressed by the magnitude of power in this tiny little body. P.J. and I both considered ourselves to be card-carrying members of the Not Easily Fazed club, but even we were occasionally rendered speechless by the instantaneous mess our darling offspring could create in the blink of an eye.

Speechless, of course, except for the impossibly high-pitched gasp of shocked panic and/or carefully modulated and colorfully imaginative G-rated curse words.

Nora was a fabulous napper- until I would decide to sneak in a quick shower. Then she'd burst into purple-faced hysterics, causing me to emerge from the bathroom with shampoo burning my eyes, one leg shaved, and a towel or whatever was closest wrapped partially around me (at times this towel was of the hand-sized variety, doing no one *any* good at all). I'd scoop her up and potentially scar her for life, what with this frightening image of someone she'd just barely begun to trust morphing into a yelping, soapy monster.

I'd nurse her on the floor and sometimes we'd cry together. Other times I'd count myself lucky to have taken such an awesome half-shower.

She developed what some in the know would term a "witching hour," kind of like a happy hour, with slightly less booze but the same amount of hysterics. The only thing that would soothe Principessa D'Yellipants was a spin in the baby sling. I'd strap this thing to me around four or five in the afternoon, and attempt to throw together dinner without royally pissing off anyone miniature. Sometimes it worked. Other times, regardless of my terrific skills in the dancing around and soothing speak department, we'd end up ordering takeout.

There were other things of which no one had informed me during my impending motherhood. Which is ironic, considering that people certainly weren't mincing words anywhere else.

Among them: Why oh *why* hadn't I purchase my nursing bras before I was actually sustaining a child? In a multitude of sizes? Granted, that wonderful woman at Macy's had told me to come back for more pregnancy bra sizing, but she didn't follow up on the nursing bra front. So I blame her.

Even if the previously purchased nursing bras are the wrong size- which, oh, they will be- that little bit of foresight will save one the acute unhappiness that a post-pregnancy bra shopping trip will undoubtedly bring. It's pretty hard to remove and try on articles of clothing while clad in strategic nursing pads. And to be effective, those pads need to be in their proper locations at all times. Which, when removed to make way for other items of boob-holdin', leave the chest with no reinforcements. And someone ends up getting a little soaky in unmentionable locales.

I've already said too much.

Do I even need to *say* that there were tears? No?

Also, that first time using one's breast pump is something for which one cannot prepare. Even *with* instructions. But allow me to offer a few key tips: Make sure that the suction function is working properly. Do not let anyone physically help you. Yes, muddle through on your own. Because, even if they're your bestest of friends, this is not a sight for audiences. And finally, if you *do* decide to get help via a quick Skype tutorial from a sibling (for instance) keep in mind that you're one screen angle/dropped blankie away from internet pornography at all times. I hope that this helps someone out there.

Besides, while nursing one's child and pumping to supplement are admirable goals, deciding to *not* pump is a good choice as well.

For the pump is evil.

P.J. and I underwent rapid-fire Parent Evolution; we never traveled anywhere without three diapers and outfits, and learned to place at least a towel's worth of (washable) padding underneath any small and digesting human being.

We also learned true fear the first night that we hooked up her monitor. Feeling that we simply had to be on top of her every sleep movement (or at least be able to lazily flick a button and see if she was stuck in the crib's bars/under an ill-advised lovie/just yelling for no reason), we purchased a monitor that featured both audio and video channels. (Also, all of the families for whom I had nannied possessed these things. I was *not* going to miss out.)

After positioning the base and screwing it onto the wall over her crib, we went back to our room to check the view. And it was lovely. A simple yet solid crib, a sheet I didn't quite remember buying, and- hey, where were the (highly inadvisable) crib bumpers patterned with the cheerfully crayoned circles? Not to mention Otto, where was Otto? And now that we were on the subject, that baby, that blanketless, lovie-less baby...

That was not our baby in the crib.

We ran back into Nora's room to find- Nora. Back to our room to find- that other kid. I watched for a few more moments, fascinated by this completely empty-except-for-a-baby crib. P.J. guessed that this chilly child (he/she of the rule-abiding parentage) lived across the street, either in an apartment or in one of the sparsely populated condos.

Eventually the other kid stirred and I panicked, shutting off our monitor. I hoped that someone was actually watching him/her. (I had a brief moment of panic; was *I* supposed to be watching that baby? Was I unwittingly on the clock?)

And after toggling the channels a few time, Chilly Child vanished, replaced by our own overly swaddled Sweaty Kid.

Soon after that, we were frightened to the core by the sound of inordinately angry and slightly bigoted voices screaming through her monitor. My first thought (ghosts) was quickly replaced by a second, slightly more rational guess: an axe murderer (with a racist bent) stomping about in the nursery.

And you know things have Gotten Real when you're wishing the ghosts would just come back.

Turns out it was just a simple case of a questionably angry tow truck driver using a CB radio to broadcast his bitter little thoughts (in front of a residence in the middle of the night). His frequency overtook the monitor's and we were blissfully privy to a short rant. Who hasn't had *that* one happen?

(In terms of Monitor Fear, however, my big sister's tale takes the cake. After installing the monitor in the bedroom of their firstborn, they turned it on and instantly heard a baby's wail. Only problem? She was still pregnant. Turns out that it was the neighbor's kiddo from down the hall, but it still freaked the bejesus out of them and convinced at least one of them that the unborn child was trying to communicate.)

After all of these technology tales o' terror, we began to debate the merits of old fashioned childcare. Namely, placing an ear against the baby's bedroom door and cautiously whispering, "You awake yet?"

My daily priorities had changed. Personal hygiene became optional, and all of those things that I scoffed at in my Nanny Life (why did it take parents *hours* to get out of the house and what was with all of the Tupperware/bottle parts on the countertops?) smacked me upside the head with my own arrogance. Apparently, being a well-rested nanny in my early twenties (with an absolute exit strategy for 5pm each day) made me stupidly optimistic about how Parenting Should Go. I mentally chuckled at Younger Me, knowing that someday she'd get hers. Other times I berated her. Once I asked her to get an amaretto stone sour and enjoy the hell out of it for me. These were private conversations, mind you. Acknowledging that you mentally pressure Younger Yourself to drink is not for all crowds.

It is important to note that, while showers themselves became optional, my quirks were still going in full force. For example, if I did indeed get to bathe, I'd prioritize shaving my armpits over conditioning my hair. My rationale was this; my armpits were usually on full display while nursing. Sure, so was (at least) one gigantic boob, but I couldn't have cared less about that by the time we had brought Nora home. There was Biological Necessity, and then there was just plain ol' Being Gross.

My dress code had drastically changed as well. My previous love of clean jeans quickly morphed into a passion for (questionably clean) sweatpants and a rainbow assortment of tank tops with the aforementioned built-in nursing capabilities.

I used to pride myself on my admirable collection of leather boots and Italian handbags. I still do. But now I wave at them from afar and enjoy fond little remembrances, kind of the way that you wonder what your junior year boyfriend is up to these days.

And I finally got it. Overly casual clothing on new mothers was nothing to scoff at, nor did it symbolize utter laziness. All it meant was that no one who might see the new Mom that day would possibly care if she matched, and also that if she had the slightest chance of taking a floor nap any time in the near future, then by God she was going to be ready for it.

On those days where we had it together enough to venture out of doors (with Nora bundled within an inch of her life and me wearing a weird mix of maternity, pre-pregnancy clothing, and something under which to hide my Don Kingesque hair) we ran into an entirely new choir of people with information to impart. These were close cousins to the Experienced Ones, but were known as the Older Generation. Their battle cry was That's Not How We Did It In My Day.

They had great deals of concern for whether or not Nora was too hot, a little chilly, or perhaps was in too direct of sunlight. This group is still heartily convinced that babies sleep best on their bellies and that a little rice, potato, or whiskey in baby's bottle will help them sleep through the night. (Which is probably true, but if anyone's gonna get whiskey before bed, it sure isn't going to be the child.)

It most likely didn't help that Nora had decided really early on that she didn't exactly care for the out of doors. Neither the sunlight nor the fresh(ish) city air did it for her. She combated both of these horrors by promptly smashing her face into a blanket or into whatever carrying contraption I had shoved her and playing possum until we were safely back inside.

That alone caused a flurry of Concerned Comments about whether or not she could breathe. And maybe I shouldn't hold her that way. Or use a blanket. (Unless perhaps I wanted to put *another* blanket on her.)

Sure, I was a relatively new mother, but I'd been a longtime member of the Doesn't Take Constructive Criticism Well club. These mothers cemented my theory that there was just no such thing as good, unsolicited advice.

Timely information was fine, a la "Oh my goodness, your

child has *just this moment* wrapped a blanket three times around her nasal passages! I leave it wholly up to you to deal with this new and strange situation!"

And then boom; step back, lady.

Jovial anecdotes are also okay, such as "My kid used to accidentally suffocate on her *own* blankie and I'd combat it by gently removing the corners from her mouth. That's just one school of thought, though, ha ha! Isn't having children *the best?*"

High five and we're out.

That last comment is especially good, specifically because it makes it seem like the two mothers are in a special, members-only club. Which is cool, because that's nothing at all like berating someone with your own personal brand of tried and true Amen Do It Now advice. And clubs are fun.

I eventually started just promising these women that, as Nora's mother, I'd *try* to keep an eye on her. At least 'til her father came home, who was also generally pretty responsible.

For some of these mothers, they were just genuinely trying to help me with The Best Way That Things Work. And I appreciated the sentiment from the hopefully good place from where it came. But I (quietly) kept in mind that, at one time, using iodine as suntan oil and letting kids rattle around the backseat of an Oldsmobile were the only ways to operate. And long ago women were also sold as property. Sure, this was nowhere near the same time period as the whole lack of seatbelts thing, but I think we can all agree that a) things change all the time, and b) *we should stop badgering the new mother.*

On occasion, Nora would fall asleep face down in her crib. Sometimes she'd even have a smallish stuffed animal clutched close to her face.

Everyone knows that this is bad. *Really* bad. (Except for the older generation of Experienced Mothers. They would approve, since you only put kids to bed on their backs if you hate them.)

But, you know what? When left in this (admittedly horrifying) position, she slept for insane chunks of time. Maybe- just maybe- she was trying to tell me that when she slept like this, she was comfortable.

My new rule of thumb became If She's Sleeping, Let Her Sleep. (Night nurses be darned!)

Do not wake her to reposition her.

Do not wake her to remove the thing attached to her fist.

And do not- under any circumstance- allow an opinionated passerby to do so, either.

I started to realize that, even on the off chance I was messing my child up for life, I should probably just go with my gut feeling. (And keep a close eye; especially with that whole mashing her face into the mattress thing she adored doing.) Perhaps the parenting/rule books were a general guideline and not a hard and fast law for each kid. Maybe attachment parenting *wasn't* a guarantee that your kid would never go to prison. And there was the slightest chance that its opposite style (which I've seen some blogs describe as I Hate My Child/Totally Hands-Off Parenting) *wasn't* a one way ticket to Emotionally Cold Adulthood.

On that note, the whole competitive parenting thing needs to wither and die. Soon, please. Parents are just so mean to (and about) other parents. And I'm sorry to say it, but it's mothers who are the meanest. There's the bottle versus breast debate. All Natural If You Actually Love Your Child versus People Who Think Everything In Moderation Is Just Fine (So Shut *Up* About High Fructose Corn Syrup, Already).

And then there's argument about where the better environment is to raise a family; city versus suburbs. Sure, folks who live in big cities want their kids to have culture and exposure. So much exposure that the kids no longer *think* of it as "exposure." Families in smaller towns want nicer homes and yards, plus the ability to walk home from their school to their nicer homes and yards. But once a new baby comes into the picture, it doesn't matter if you live in a city, a town, or on the surface of the moon. Because during the first year of your kid's life, the amount of time you'll spend doing all of those convenient and culturally awesome things will be pretty negligible. It'll actually be akin to a long weekend trip visiting the city from your farmstead in Iowa.

So, with the smallish exception of Starbucks runs and proximity to Gymboree classes, even *you* won't know if you reside in a major metropolitan area or the tiniest of 'villes; you simply live in your house. (So you'd better like that house. Perhaps invest in a really, really decent home inspection? Just a suggestion.)

Another Mompiphany: No matter what I did, it was quite possible that I would still eff up my child in some minor way. This was actually slightly comforting. I contented myself with the fact that she *would* have quirks because of my choices, and she *would* blame me for a myriad of techniques that I failed or failed not to do. And she might even (and here's the crazy part) eventually do stuff and become things that had nothing to do with me or my attempts whatsoever.

This realization was actually rather freeing, as it gave me permission to blend common sense, personal preference, and the actual needs of my actual child as I raised her. As long as I never, ever, admitted these (wildly incorrect) choices out loud in public.

After the freak show of things that had happened to my body during the pregnancy, I figured that I had seen just about the worst that Mother Nature can throw at a woman.

Then came the Postpartum Body.

My hair, which just weeks before had been so gloriously thick and full, was now swirling down the drain in big ol' clumps. The stuff that remained broke off and split quite unprettily. And frankly, the potential damage to the plumbing was way more worrisome than possible bald spots. (This is yet another clear differentiation between my carefree renter-dom and my stressed out homeownitude. The former could always call the landlord to fix the drain, but hair was a commodity. The latter prefers to keep the Home Depot runs to a minimum, so let's just wear a head scarf.)

The belly that had been stretched to capacity (even for a deceptively small child) was now deflated and marred by the arrival of stretch marks in a few places. These marks, mind you, had come at quite a shock mere days before Nora showed up. Even though my strict regimen of daily cocoa butter threatened to slide me right out of the operating room, those pesky lines managed to creep in at the last minute. And if I thought they had looked less than lovely on my mammoth belly, they really didn't do the belly sag any favors.

"But it's all for the child, and isn't that worth it?"

Yes, Earth Mamas, yes. Your oft-repeated chorus is rather true; I'd rather have this darling kid than abs of steel (sigh), but can't there be a middle ground between Gold Coast Barbie and Deflated Jabba the Hut?

Someone even had the gall to ask me for whom I needed to look good, now that I had my baby. Yow. (I guess those folks believe that a future Baby #2 would happen while all parties were wearing blindfolds?)

But looking good came at a distant second to feeling

good. And for a while there, I most definitely was *not*. C-section pain aside, I was plagued with the really common side effect of trapped gas inside of the chest and abdominal cavity. (Yes, this is a real thing, and *it is terrifying*.) It manifested itself by stabbing me in the neck, shoulders, and back, sometimes giving me an Indian Sunburn any time I stood up for the first few weeks of Nora's life.

So I refrained from standing up.

This may be why when P.J., Nora, and I took our first family walk to the park a week after Nora was born (a mere four city blocks away) I slowly hunched and shuffled my way there, gripping her stroller like I was about to hit a hooligan with my walker.

I made another classic newbie mother mistake two months after having Nora. Since my maternity pants had been bagging at the hips and butt, I figured it was high time to get some new clothes. Clothes that would reflect my rapidly changing style, my status as a new (yet refreshingly hip) mother, and my propensity for lying down whenever the opportunity presented itself. Obviously I wasn't yet able to fit into my pre-pregnancy size jeans; nor did I expect to. I wasn't *crazy*.

So I went shopping.

Have you ever tried to muffle your tears over the failure to yank jeans over your knees, while the salesperson asks if everything's okay in there? (Everything clearly was *not* okay anywhere in the vicinity of "there.")

And here I was, thinking my major hurdle would be to button pants around my bizarrely sized belly. Apparently, even the region between my shins and thighs gained weight and changed sizes during pregnancy. This was unexpected.

And I'm certain that this will make me sound downright one hundred and two years old, but what the heck happened to jeans? (Or dungarees, as my mother used to call them. Okay, now we're getting a little Laura Ingalls Wilder. At least I didn't refer to them as "slacks.")

Not that the blame can be placed solely on the style of jeans I tried on (after all, *they* didn't force bags of tacos into my salty hands) but still, there wasn't an impressive range of styles from which to choose. There were the skinnies. The tapered skinnies. The hip-hugger, don't breathe, sassy script on the butt skinnies. I actually carried a pair of these into the changing room. Three sizes up, of course, but I grabbed a pair. I've never liked my rear end to be advertising for any brand or catch phrase (Single n' Sassy! Can't Afford This! Why Are You Staring At My Butt?), but I wanted to stay relevant.

Helpful hint: If you have to attempt relevancy, you've already lost.

Regardless, these didn't fit. But neither did the voluminous jeans that allowed for front-butt as well as classic rear. I kind of wanted to take some of the excess fabric from the "full-figured" options and paste them onto the skinnies.

I had to come to terms with the fact that my new shape was downright "onion;" bulbous and tapered. And with my decision to never approach anything marketed as remotely "Mom Jean," I was stuck with cinched elastic-waisted maternity khakis and yoga pants (even though there was a decided lack of yoga going on in the household).

People kept telling me to take my time and not to worry. After all, "nine months on, nine months off." But, as kind as everyone was being, I really didn't need any more fuel for my laziness fire.

That's how people end up in elastic pants and "Hang In There, Kitten!" sweatshirts for a painfully long time. Like, into retirement. (Another sweatshirt I didn't want to find myself wearing: "It's One Of Those Days." Why are things so rough for graphic cats?)

After a couple of weeks of self-imposed isolation (read: once the good drugs ran out) we started returning calls and acknowledging that, yes, other folks might want to meet this much-hyped child of ours.

Our same friends that were just now cleaning paint and varnish from their hair were, not surprisingly, the same folks who showed up with baked goods, casseroles, and salad fixings. (Really close pals brought chilled bottles of Riesling.) All of these gestures were totally unexpected yet appreciated. After all, we certainly didn't need anything (other than a solid six hours of sleep) but knowing that there were pals who cared really made a difference. It's always good to have the type of friends who would let the cops into your house after a month or so of no word. Especially since they'd likely be the ones to find the bodies.

Yeah, I watch TV.

But, cementing my ungrateful frienditude, I silently made a list of does and don'ts for dealing with tweaked-out new parents. Tops on this list was the hard n' fast rule of visiting the new family for no more than an hour. I found that even the best of pals would warrant clean sweatpants (on my part) and a general sweeping-out (on the house's part). I had been too much of a neat freak for so long that I couldn't relax with company, knowing that the house was in total chaos. Not to mention my frightful self, regardless of the state of my armpits.

And, lamely enough, I just didn't have it in me to entertain, even if the only "entertaining" expected of me was to open the door and make small talk with the friends who were making/bringing dinner.

Our new favorite dinner ritual had evolved into sitting in front of the TV and planting our faces into whatever warmed-up dish someone had lovingly prepared for us. It wasn't a sight for all audiences. (Although I expect it would make an exceptional birth control P.S.A.)

I also promised myself I'd never show up empty-handed and expect the family whom I was visiting to host me for the evening. We actually had a few people show up, purportedly "for dinner," but who stared at me blankly once they arrived and inquired as to what we'd be having. I think a good rule of thumb should be that you can't expect someone to cook for you if their day's only meal has consisted of a half sandwich eaten over the sink.

I mean, sure, I'm a mother now, but I'm not *your* mother!

Midway up this list was to never express a desire to just come over and "hold the baby." I didn't need anyone to hold the baby. *I* wanted to hold the baby. I have peed myself in joy (and incontinence) when friends offered to wipe down my countertops, lint roll the cat hair from the sofa, and tuck me in for a mandatory nap with said baby while they Windexed the floss spit from the bathroom mirror. (Now *that's* a thank-you card Hallmark hasn't yet cornered.)

A newborn baby sleeps roughly 37 hours a day, especially when cuddled. It's that other stuff that becomes a pain in the butt.

For the first time since the fourth grade, I realized that a homemade coupon book is truly the world's most perfect gift.

Another thing we hadn't counted on was the transition of my persona from New Girlfriend/Old Pal's Wife to Motherly Mom in the eyes of my husband's friends. Now, a good bunch of them were liberal, modern men who were only slightly weirded out by their friend's new lifestyle. But there were definitely a couple of guys who could not wrap their minds around the fact that P.J. was now a Dad.

Or that his wife was now a Mom.

One who breastfed.

In the middle of the kitchen.

And let me just tell you, there are few things more socially awkward than a person trying his hardest not to look at something. Or two somethings. So my options were to choose between pretending ignorance during a state of super awareness, or to nurse the kid in the other room. And since Nora was a fan of cluster feeding every ten to fifteen minutes, this meant I had zero time with our company.

Which, let's face it, wasn't full of stimulating conversation if everyone was just staring at my boobs, anyhow.

On the flip side of this chesty coin: Have you ever stopped to realize that when you caress or smooch a nursing baby's head, you're pretty much caressing or smooching your friend's breasts? I think we should all take a second to realize that.

Even in my whiny state of self-righteous sleepiness, I realized that I had it pretty good. A long maternity leave, a husband who insisted on getting and changing the baby each time she awoke in the night (which may have been *his* brush with temporary insanity), and a relatively easy new child.

That said, unless there's a staff of day nannies and night nurses at one's beck and call, most new parents are inevitably going to be tired. I actually knew some of the mothers who would employ this sort of staff; they always complained of being tired, too. Proving either that a) children are exhausting to have in one's home, or b) that people with money are no happier than they ought to be.

I had been feeling pretty proud of myself and my varying states of late-night alertness while nursing Nora. P.J. and I would high-five each other and congratulate ourselves on being grownup parents. At 3am, this often felt like a really bizarre game of pretend.

This confidence lasted roughly a week, until I jolted awake to find P.J.'s head tipped backwards over the headboard in mid-snore and Nora's ankles clasped to my boob. Her gaping and confused mouth was in the general area of the mattress and, from her disappointed cries, I could tell that she hadn't actually been fed by me or anyone else.

Her ankles were well supported, however.

My nighttime parenting fails were accompanied by the American version of *The Office*. It had been on the air for a couple of years by this point, but it really took a few marathon viewing sessions to truly make me a super fan. And there's nothing quite as surreal as slamming through six seasons of a show between the hours of midnight and five a.m. The dreams alone can make you question your sanity. The imagined relationships that you've forged with characters can absolutely tip you over the edge into Crazy Town. And when Jim and Pam had their daughter right after we had ours? Forget the fact that they are fictitious beings, I cried. And wished I could invite them for a play date. Because they would understand me. I wagered that they didn't have a night nurse, either.

Mainlining such a stylized show (in the middle of the night, no less) also had the repercussion of changing my speech patterns. I began responding in quips, one-liners, and snarky asides. Sometimes while the show was still playing on my TV. Other times when I was alone in the house.

My language skills and former eloquence had been reduced to such mush since Nora's arrival that I'm sure P.J. found this foray into television insanity a slight improvement.

During these nursing and rocking sessions, I also wondered about the possible ramifications on Nora. I'm willing to place money on her future Pavlovian response to the opening theme song of that show.

Maybe she'll just have a strong dairy craving.

CHAPTER THIRTEEN

(Love, love, love.)

The first few weeks of having Nora home weren't all about awkward nudity, aborted showers, and mentally berating acquaintances, however. Far from it. There were also bursts of endorphins and dizzying amounts of love like we'd never experienced. Obnoxiously gushy, but undeniably true.

Back when P.J. and I first met, I never doubted how much he liked me. But I couldn't possibly have expected the reaction to his newborn daughter. If his love for me was as tall as Chicago's Sears/Willis Tower, then his love for Nora goes from the tip of the Willis to the moon and back to the lowest immeasurable depth of the ocean where whale sharks live. And how could I be jealous of that? No sane person can envy a brand-new love *for a being that you've created*. It's just not possible. You can be impressed, sure. But not envious.

Maybe it has something to do with the fact that Nora could've been P.J.'s twenty-eight years younger and female clone. Aside from the obvious (and impossibly wide) mouth, they had the same cheekbones, toes with a tendency to overlap, even eyebrows that slightly wisped up at their ends. She's a towhead, the same as baby P.J., whereas I've always been positively dark. (Unless we're including my slightly unfortunate foray into the world of Sun-In at thirteen years of age, which resulted in a glamorous orange hue with a distinctly crunchy texture. But let's go ahead and not include that.)

"Good for you," I've told P.J. "You deserve a doppelganger after all of your hard work."

Which, in all actuality, he probably does. Because putting up for me for thirty-nine weeks of gestation, a crabby hospital stay, and the chaotic first few weeks home with our child should come with a few merit badges.

The only thing I can claim on Nora is the budding temper than emerges during her middle of the night feedings. There's a look in those dark little eyes that suggests perhaps we can speed up the diapering/public nudity process, yes? And *maybe* get one of us on a boob a tad faster?

Sometimes when P.J. would hand her to me after swaddling Nora within an inch of her life, I would liken her face to a miniature Nosferatu. Her tiny fists, recently Houdini'd from her blankets, would be balled up at her cheeks and her angry eyes would dart back and forth until she was sated. Then she would turn back into a sweetly dreaming porcelain doll once again.

I realize it's not exactly poetry to compare one's infant to an infamous vampire, but I'm just calling it like I see it. (I still wanted to eat her face with a spoon, tiny monster or not.)

As for me, I knew that I was in a new kind of love as well. My very definition of time had changed, even beyond the obvious "there's not enough of it." During the pregnancy, I found myself rounding up my answer whenever people would ask how far along I was. Eight weeks became two months, even though P.J. would gently remind me how the weeks/months difference worked. Advice: do not ever correct your pregnant wife. Of course eight weeks isn't exactly two months. But if she wants to say that thirty three weeks is close to nine months (which, you know, it *kinda* is) or that the sea is purple; well then, fella, you best get on your Agreeable Hat.

However, as soon as Nora turned four weeks old, well, that wasn't a month at all. That was simply four weeks.

I wanted time to slow down. Actually, I wanted it to stop. As much as I complained my way through my imagined eighteen months of pregnancy (like an elephant!), I reveled my way through every single moment of early motherhood.

I didn't mind the late night feedings. Actually, I looked forward to them, as I really found myself missing Nora all the way across the room in her bassinet (and P.J. was *not* keen on waking her just so I could say "hi"). Plus, if we went too long between nighttime visits, my chest would threaten to explode with the weight of my over-full boobs.

I now started to (partially) understand the Just Waits- and I resented them strongly for it. When I was a kid, I used to have moments of extreme sadness while opening my own birthday presents. The idea that I would never be further away from opening my gifts as I was at that very second just about destroyed me. (I was a very emotional child. Perhaps that office closet would've been better used as a therapist's couch.)

But the Sunday evening sadness and the birthday anticipation? That was nothing compared to sitting and holding Nora, watching her sleep. I'd feel her wiggle against my shoulder in the way that meant she was threatening to wake up and shatter this fleeting peace. I'd meditate on her impossibly small face, thinking about all that I knew of her in such a short amount of time, yet realizing that it was a drop in the bucket of what she'd become.

P.J. laughed as he saw me quietly weeping on our child's bald head one night.

"You're thinking about how you love her too much, aren't you?"

It briefly made me wish for one of those husbands who remained utterly unaware of their wives' plethora of Feelings, leaving them to irrationally cry in peace. But his laughter was the understanding kind as well, since he knew that it had been merely the blink of an eye since we had met over scripts. Held hands across a lopsided and shellacked booth at the Pick Me Up Café, ordering completely unnecessary caffeine at 1am (and laughing like loons at how cool we each thought the other to be). Began a grocery routine that included "our" products like Cheetos and the good kind of orange juice. And chose a home based on the fatefulness of what the current Chicago listings were.

And if those things could just zip on past, then *this* moment, this peaceful innocence with a newborn; well, I was sure I could just kiss that time goodbye. I already missed her. I thought about how I'd feel when she went off to school (and then college!), coming home briefly with friends and boyfriends, eventually getting married and moving eight hundred miles from home. Nora wasn't even a month old yet, and I had already relegated her to a Christmas card and the occasional collect call (which I'm fairly certain no longer even exists).

Those thoughts paved the way to ones where we all would grow older. I informed P.J. that he and I were definitely going to die someday. My heart ached so much I thought it would rip itself out of my chest and thud to the floor. This wonderful little person, so new and so dependent on us, how could we leave her alone in this lonely world? I missed her. And I grieved for her missing us. This thought sent me spiraling into such unhappiness that I accidentally woke Nora with my heaving sobs.

P.J. soothed me, soothed Nora, and reassured everyone involved that no one had to die. (As irrational as that is, it's good to hear every now and again.) He promised me that we had buckets of time, including this very moment which I was squandering with my Feelings. Then he kissed Nora and said something that stopped my heart with its utter simplicity and beauty and mind-boggling truth:

"Just think…there are others that we haven't even met

yet."

So there was time. Even though there was *no time*, there was time. I was content to Just Wait.

Besides openly weeping over my child, a few other things emerged that I was actually quite good at; among them anything that resembled playing House, the game I loved most dearly as a kid. Folding miniature laundry and laying out her ridiculously small outfits didn't seem like the chore it could be when dealing with adult-sized shirts and socks.

This was good, because the girl knew how to rack up dirty pairs of pants.

I liked sanitizing her bottles and lining up her feeding accouterments. Stacking diapers and changing bassinet sheets. Rearranging books and toys for optimal viewing from the crib.

And yes, I realize that the majority of my skill set had very little to do with the actual child and was more about the touching of her possessions.

Since she was such a fan of the baby sling, I really liked just walking around with her stuck to me all day. It wasn't an Attachment Parenting thing (and it also wasn't a Non-Attachment Parenting thing); it was just convenient. Whereas the former choice is all about the needs of the child, my rational for wearing her was all about the needs of my hands to actually hold and do stuff. It was surprising how much I could get done with a newly secured baby appendage. It was also exceptional weight training and decent cardio if I included a few sets on the stairs. (I had found myself missing the previously wedged couch, if only for the potential added calorie scorch.)

The added bonus of getting a ton of stuff done while wearing Nora was that, when she needed to nap, I could occasionally allow myself to rest with her for a bit.

There are few things nicer than having a warm and snuggly infant napping directly under one's chin. It's an anti-depressant, sleep aid, and endorphin booster all in one.

It's also really easy to convince yourself that the child will only nap well if cuddled like that; and who doesn't want their child to be a good napper? People who hate their kids, that's who. (These are things that I told myself as I took my third nap of the day. *For the child.*)

I started seriously questioning how people could leave their kids for any great length of time. And it blew my mind that there existed in this world people who viewed their babies as inconveniences. Or really, anything short of absolutely, miraculously wonderful.

And yes, I had been this prone to hyperbole even before post-baby adrenaline/post-hospital medications.

Extenuating circumstances and financial concerns aside, I knew far too many parents who were ambivalent about the day to day realities of their actual children. It boggled, because (and here's another obnoxious realization) babies are an actual miracle. I knew this, of course, but I didn't *know* this. It's like when smug parents tell their single friends how "having a baby changes everything." It does, of course, but even when their friends are nodding and agreeing, they can't possibly get the full magnitude. It's just one of those things that can't fully be internalized until you're in the 3am trenches, covered in God-knows-what, and screaming, *"Everything has changed!"*

Allow me a grand assumption: We all know where babies come from. Hopefully.

But I'm pretty sure that every new parent has that postpartum moment of *this child was not even here before I decided to have her. (Or have fate decide for me. Whatever.)* More mind-blowingly crazy was the realization that I had grown this being's toenails and hair follicles and lungs. Regardless of my own inability to properly operate a Bunsen burner in sophomore year chemistry, my genetic makeup instinctively knew how to create another's genetic makeup. (Yes. These thoughts went through my mind months *after* I had grown and birthed a baby. Yes they did.)

And since I already adored this Bitsy bucket of 50/50 DNA more than anything I had ever known, how could I possibly ever leave her? Even to go to the store?

I began seriously questioning the profession of nannies. I couldn't imagine how new parents were able to leave their children with relative strangers. Keep in mind, I adored my jobs. And the children for whom I cared. And was oh-so grateful to the parents who trusted me with their babies and paid me gobs of money to love their kids while they themselves worked and traveled and did wonderful things outside of their homes. I could not, however, connect *that* to *this*. It was not the same thing. It was not the same thing at all.

And let's not even broach the subject of taking one's child outside without a team of medical experts. There are cars out there. And trains and guns and strangers who wish to touch your child directly on their mucus membranes. This doesn't even include the frightening people who wish to talk at you. It almost makes you miss the pre-pregnancy Death Sentencers, doesn't it? Almost. At least then, the child was safely ensconced.

It made me wonder how I could ever willingly leave this game of Roulette to childcare professionals who had never even birthed my daughter. Which was a mighty narrow group of people, this I realize.

Piggybacking on my Stranger Danger worries was my growing horror of anything germy. I had tended towards the borderline OCD at times, but my fears were now becoming a completely unchecked germophobia of positively Howard Hughes proportions. Living in a city, I was well aware of how disgusting things could become. But the full magnitude of how gross humanity was really hit me once I realized how much filth I was inadvertently shoving into Nora's face. We're talking things that touched the kid, touched her room, and touched me touching her room.

Inadvisably, I read an emailed article that suggested how when folks wore shoes inside a home, they were actually trekking in everything that their town had to offer. Sidewalk urine. Pet excrement. Garbage can overflow. It went on to detail how these traces of awfulness could make their way into your bathrooms, your kitchens, *your bed*.

Shortly thereafter, shoes were kindly yet loudly requested to be left by the door.

Then I read that doorknobs and remote controls carry (and cultivate!) more germs than your average toilet seat. And while I wasn't sure if my bathroom's toilet was more or less yucky than average, I was quite certain of one thing: People really needed to stop forwarding me emails.

I couldn't wash my hands nearly enough. Target didn't stock enough antibacterial hand lotion. And the countertop toy sanitizer- easily the most obnoxiously indulgent invention for this generation of parents- was running constantly.

I accidentally melted Nora's newly received and much-loved Sophie teething giraffe by steaming the thing into sanitary silence. Sure, giraffes are normally quiet as a bunch, but I actually fused the squeak box to its throat. (Apparently, natural rubber is a delicate substance. Darn you, conscientious parenting! This never would've happened with a BPA toy!)

And in that vein, things that I used to think were just nice ideas were now insane obsessions. Back in the early 80s, the cups and spoons I used as a baby were *not* BPA-free. People didn't know what was or wasn't in their kids' items except for, you know, plastic. And plastic was easily washable. So that was that.

But when it came to my own kid? Suddenly I was reading the labels on her rubber ducks. Ducks! The idea that my daughter would become exposed to cancer-causing toxins during her routine (hypoallergenic and organic) bubble bath was my new worst fear.

I became fixated on the idea of cleaning with vinegar and lemon juice. (Not the most effective of bathroom cleansers, but it does make a stellar vinaigrette.) And as much as I knew in my heart of hearts that germs were good for the kid (and also that I was single-handedly contributing to a race of mutated super germs) I couldn't stop washing my hands nor ruining my daughter's possessions.

No one ever promised that rationality would hit once I became a mother.

All of these mental issues with which to grapple were downright exhausting. Is it any wonder why I couldn't finish anything on my maternity leave checklist? Stage plays did not get penned. Handwritten thank-you notes were not mailed. The shower stall did not get wiped down, not even once. The brain cells required to keep Nora alive and, you know, panic over potentially inconsequential and irrelevant Things That Could

Happen left very little drive for other things.

Like, ahem, romance.

So I'd like to offer up a PSA on behalf of all new mothers that concerns such laughable concepts as Personal Space, Physical Boundaries, and Energy Levels.

If the stars are all somehow aligned and a) the child is sleeping peacefully in her bassinet, b) the house is in a relatively ordered state, and c) the new mother comes to bed in her sassiest of fleecy cat pajamas, feel free to give her a foot rub and a snuggle.

If, however, she's crawling into bed wearing her retainers, yesterday's nursing tank, a burp cloth over one shoulder, and can't remember if she just popped a Norco or a baby suppository…

…Then for the love of the baby Jesus, give her at least an hour of face-planting before someone needs anything related to any one of her body parts. (The retainer should always be a pretty fierce indicator.)

This is just a polite suggestion.

I am highly aware that I may be the only female for whom the following is applicable, but somehow I don't think I'm alone; there is nothing in the universe more romantic, sexy, or mood-setting than a boudoir with a made bed, fluffed pillows, and nary a basket of laundry to be seen. The room should, however, possess an abundance of soft light streaming through (recently dusted) wooden blinds. A soft breeze wouldn't hurt, either.

On second thought, forget the romance. This is the perfect storm for a nap. But maybe after the nap, if all of those conditions are still set, maybe then.

However, half the battle is actually showing up. Or state of mind. Or knowing. I can never remember which. What was the one that G.I. Joe said? Go with one of the other two.

So sometimes you've just got to fake it until you make it. With clothing, that is.

Sock size doesn't really change too much during and after pregnancy, and footwear is hardly the sexiest of bedroom attire. Unless you're talking about a superbly gorgeous pair of stacked leather boots; but no, that doesn't help with the everyday. There are too many stairs in my home for sexy shoes on a Tuesday. (Besides, I'd already decided to ban indoor shoe-wearing for all of eternity.)

But attractive underwear can make all the difference. Sure, these yoga pants are covered in unrecognizable substances and have never even *seen* the inside of a gym, but the layer underneath? I'm a pretty, pretty princess.

Trust me, this works. And then you'll feel awesome

enough for extracurricular activities, such as simultaneously falling asleep atop a basket of your mutual child's laundry. (Ah, passion.)

Don't, however, make the rookie mistake I did at my ol' standby Victoria's Secret. These (previously lovely) folks, for some strange reason, offer nothing in the way of maternity underthings or nursing bras. Why do you not view motherhood as a Sexy Little Thing, Victoria? Here's a secret for you, one that I've recently imparted to the Earth Mamas; subsequent children do not come from a lacy and bedazzled stork.

CHAPTER FOURTEEN

(I'm not a hermit. Or hobbit. I can't remember which.)

Even though I had very little to show for having had such a lengthy time off (besides a healthy and generally cheerful infant, which cannot be discounted), I definitely took the time to regain some semblance of my senses. This also prevented me from going all Emily Dickinson on the world, which was becoming more and more of a possibility with each passing day. We had a lot in common, Em n' me. Residing in Amherst for a bit, having a general distaste for leaving the house, and trying to write in said house. Really, the only major difference was the whole "giving birth to a child in a major metropolitan setting" thing. That's pretty much it.

Despite the occasional ten minute forays into the sunshine/germs/crush of opinionated people, there were times when we all actually had to go out into the world. Like to the doctor's office once a week for the first eighty months of her life. These appointments are routine, set in stone, and decided upon the instant you give birth. They weigh your kid, they measure your kid, and then they ask when you're going to set up the appointments for tuberculosis shots.

Can we touch upon an extremely polarizing issue for a second? From the moment Nora was born, I had to make decisions about whether or not to give her the Hepatitis vaccine. Vitamin K. Some other stuff that was most likely included in the cornucopia of drugs she had gotten from *my* bloodstream. But even with my love for delicious painkillers, I had momentary pause about all of the vaccines.

That doesn't mean that I didn't get her vaccinated. Just that I felt badly about it. There has been so much press in recent years about alternate vaccination schedules or even foregoing them altogether. And I am no doctor. This cannot be stressed enough: *I am not a medical professional, nor have I ever attempted to impersonate one (save for that one time in an improv sketch).*

But regardless of how little my child is, or how much I think it's going to hurt her, or even with my lack of knowledge regarding future medical research, I know this much: I do not wish for my child to be the reason that polio makes a comeback. And we *do* know this: vaccines prevent polio from making a comeback.

I get it, I really do. Because seeing two-day-old Nora get a long needle in the thigh broke my heart in fifty places. And it was even worse at her week-old appointment. Triple that for the two and four month appointments. On the sixth month, as P.J. and I held a sobbing Nora down for her second of four shots that visit, I fully acknowledged to the cosmos that I was a jerky monster who didn't deserve happiness. And P.J. had to look away so that no one saw his Man Tears.

But recently, multiple infants in Chicago died from whooping cough. *Whooping cough.* That's like opening the

Tribune one morning and reading that your neighbor was trampled to death by a Stegosaurus. *This should not still be happening.*

Even though I feel pretty strongly about this one, I understand that others may make decisions that work better for their families. And this is totally cool. But if your kid has polio, I'm probably not going to let her share a juice box with Nora. Just a heads up.

Then there were times that I felt like a complete derelict because I abandoned Nora for non-crucial events of personal fulfillment. For instance, I left her at a mere three weeks of age. I almost called Child Services on myself.

It was to attend a play reading. And I was gone for two and a half hours. And the play in question was one that I had penned. So it wasn't like I left her naked in a corn field to go to Vegas or anything. And the person with whom I "left" her was none other than her father, whose credentials checked out but you really can never be too careful with childcare.

My sister was my date to the event, and she had the joyous honor of hearing me kvetch about how much I ached for my child while we were still pulling out of the garage.

This was the first time since I had really *known* about Nora that she hadn't been within my sight (or hearing or feeling) for any real length of time; it was beyond strange. I wasn't sure what do with all of this extra mobility. It also led me to question such things like, "Am I wearing pants?" My sister informed me that, since I had chosen a skirt, I was actually *not*. But in an appropriate way.

The reading itself went quite well, although I was half-hallucinating from lack of sleep, not to mention a healthy dose of unfounded Nora Panic. When a guy asked a question in the post-show talkback session, I started to answer him as intelligently as I knew how. Then I paused. Then I thought some more and realized I had absolutely *no recollection* as to what his initial question was. I finished my answer with that honest statement.

"I'm so sorry, I forgot what you originally asked me. Also, I can't remember the sentence I uttered before this one."

It garnered some pity applause. (I will *take* it!) When my sister and I returned home shortly thereafter, I celebrated with half of a beer. And reminisced fondly about how I used to (metaphorically) wear lampshades. And (literally) win dance-offs atop bars with Def Leppard on the jukebox.

Ah, youth/last summer.

Not a lot of our friends had had kids yet, so there was definitely some new territory through which we needed to wade.

For starters, people couldn't understand why we were suddenly missing every single artistic fundraiser, show opening, and thirty dollar, all-you-can-drink bar event. Saying that we were tired, broke, tired, had a sick baby, or were tired all seemed to be cop-outs. And on the rare occasion where we did get a babysitter? We'd cab it to a shindig, spend money on drinks or food, taxi home, and then pay the sitter. Our total tab for evening could easily top a hundred bucks for just a few hours. All this was to prove- for two hours- that we weren't lame, when in actuality, thinking these thoughts while out and about only furthered our lameness. We started doing everyone a favor and stayed home, leaving them to their youthful endeavors of "fun." Exceptions to our early bedtimes included weddings, holidays, or unexpected trips to Target pharmacy.

Because there is something damn freeing about driving solo to a drugstore in the middle of the night (a.k.a. 9pm). You actually feel like the Eagles' *Hotel California* was penned about you and your penchant for highway drivin'. Nothing slowing you down, except for the occasional side street speed bump. Not a care in the world, except for getting to the pharmacy before they closed or having to deal with the constantly disapproving pharmacy team member.

I really missed my friends. There were a few exceptional pals who went way above and beyond in terms of putting in the effort, but a lot of friends drifted away. I couldn't entirely blame them; I had become a messy, exhausted, questionably clean gal with tunnel vision for her child. Temporarily gone were the late-night excursions to The Wiener's Circle, after work beer gardens, and focused conversation.

Parenting can be lonely and I knew this going in. Even with the explosion of online support sites and mothers' groups, nothing really replaces actual face time with your good friends. The truth is, unless you know people with young kids, you're in for a long haul until your child is the right age to start attending classes. Some of these start at six months, but still; that's a long six months before you can strike up that first awkward conversation with another parent over soy lattes.

Because meeting new parent friends is like dating. It's uncomfortable and thrilling and, if you threw in a few strobe lights and Bon Jovi tracks, it'd be just like the Free Skate at the roller rink. *"Will someone just please hold my hand to Livin' On A Prayer,"* I found myself wanting to yell at the playground.

So P.J. and I clung to our very small group of friends who already had little kids and had conversations that went a lot like this:

"I'm tired." "Me too!"

"Blah blah my house is filthy." "I may actually be wearing someone else's dinner."

"I can't manage to get to the grocery store today." "I'm impressed that you're wearing actual clothing."

"You're a superwoman." "You look put together *all the time.*"

"I can't talk right now- my child is stuck somewhere." "I totally understand."

Friendships have been based on way less.

Speaking of hitting the open road, we decided to take our recently confident show outta town. So Nora had her first road trip. A six hour jaunt from Chicago to Cincinnati for Thanksgiving, to be precise.

P.J. and I packed more gear for our twenty inch child than she could possibly have needed in a year abroad. But packing our diaper factory's worth of Huggies and enough blankets to swaddle a bison was just the beginning.

We had made the mistake of buying one of those large rearview mirrors that allowed us to see Nora every step of the drive. This meant that we were now staring at her for every inch of the drive. And after a few glimpses of what we termed The Saddest Face Known To Mankind (and having not yet crossed the state line, a mere half an hour away), P.J. suggested that we pull over.

This was new. P.J., whom again, was *very fond of me*, generally allowed me one pee break somewhere in the middle of Indiana on these trips home to see his family. If I complained about my imminent urinary tract infection, I'd get a stern remonstration to stop drinking so much water and/or hazelnut coffee with those Mini Moo creamers. All in the interest of "making good time," even though- again- not since freshman year Track has anyone timed me for anything.

But Nora was feeling sad? Pull it over, friend. Go nurse her. Does she need a diaper or a swaddle? Some French fries? Affordable gas at the Flying J?

During a bout of Nora's tears, he even suggested that *he* sit in the back with her while *I* drove. And as the only way P.J.'s not in the driver seat is if he's tied up in the trunk, I knew we were all having some serious Feelings.

There was even an ill-advised nursing session in the backseat while our car careened down I-65. (Attention Child Services: Nora was fine, all strapped in nice as you please in her seat. *I* was the one kneeling over the car seat with a blankie over both of our heads and various body parts. *Hello*, truckers.)

I can easily say that it was the strangest thing that I've ever done in the backseat of any vehicle. Least amount of clothing, too.

And I do not recommend this, for a variety of reasons besides the whole "you're half nudie in a car" thing. Such as, oh; it's illegal, and despite your best of intentions, the hungry and distressed infant will neither be soothed nor sated by your stressed form threatening to crush her at high speeds.

Even with the backseat peep show extravaganza, we still managed to tack on an extra hour and a half to the drive. My husband didn't care.

I think he preferred road-tripping with Nora, even if she added so much travel time. (Over an *hour*! Seriously. If I had wasted that much of "our" time, he would've beaten me to death with a Big Gulp.)

But, again, she resembles him a ton. That helps in the tolerance department. Also, she rarely badgered him about roadside attractions like dairy farms, outlet malls, and Cracker Barrels. (But listen, if I can't enjoy a bowl of cinnamon apples while sitting on a humongous rocking chair and pretending to be all Old Time-y, then what is the point of driving someplace in a car?)

Private moments of questionable parenting are one thing, but the first time you display it for all to see is really one for the scrapbook. Displaying my techniques, I mean.

Once we arrived in Cincinnati, all of my purported parenting acumen fled. It may have had something to do with the fact that I almost offed my daughter in a Catholic church, right in full view of the entirety of my in-law family.

The scene: two of our nephews' baptisms. I had planned and over-packed the event to a frightening degree. A pretty (and weather-appropriate dress). A backup dress. A sunhat *and* a snow hat. A few light blankies, in case anyone needed in-pew nursing. A couple of the wooden toys I'm forever foisting upon her. And more diapers than would be needed for an adult's toilet demands. Not bad for a one hour service. I felt ready.

And Nora? Well, being the darling baby that she is, she slept from the moment we placed her in the car seat until we were safely back at the homestead. You'd think that, by being asleep for the duration of the whole thing, it would have eased my mind a little, but no. I've never been exceptional at leaving well enough alone, and this day (with my duffel bag of gear, no less) was no different.

I worried that she was getting drafty on the floor beside me in that chilly little bundled car seat. So I lifted her up and placed the car seat sideways onto the pew where, you know, it's a balmy two degrees warmer, and continued to watch the church proceedings. We remained like that for about ten minutes or so, when I swear to God *out of nowhere* her seat lurched forward and wedged itself between the pew and the rail.

The clatter echoed throughout the church and precisely nine billion pairs of eyes turned to reproach me with horror.

I made a lame joke about how I clearly was going to need to keep her in her car seat until she was twelve years old. For safety, ha ha.

Not one person laughed.

Thankfully, she had been securely strapped into her seat and didn't even stir. Or I had rendered her momentarily unconscious. Either way, she was fine.

Once my heartbeat returned to its normal pace and people stopped outwardly viewing me as some kind of potential baby murderer, I realized that my initial reaction to my child's motion had been: Ghosts. (They are frickin' *everywhere*.)

Soon thereafter came the season of Christmas. Since we had clearly rocked the driving and flinging about of our child in the Midwest, we felt more than ready to take on air travel to the East Coast.

Except for the fact that all of those excessive things which had been tidily packed into the Passat's ample trunk now had to be checked and weighed and hefted.

And proof of documentation for Nora was stricter than if we had been trying to sneak her across the border. I found this slightly disconcerting. My thought was this: If anyone is actually stupid enough to *want* to travel with a small child, then I think we should just go ahead and let them do it. Even in the case of actual criminals, flying with a baby might just be punishment enough.

There was more than one conversation questioning whether or not my child was under the age of two, and thusly would require her own in-flight seat. I generally just gestured wildly towards Nora who, at eight weeks, was the size of a small Pomeranian. A super tiny one. So once we got Nora her own Lap Baby boarding pass (flashing her teensy tiny identification along the way) we got to experience a security check with an infant.

We had to remove her shoes. Which were actually socks with shoes painted on. They cared not; the socks apparently looked suspicious. She needed to be removed from the cotton sling in which she was bundled. Then the sling and her coat needed to be scanned. Strangely, they didn't check her diaper, which- if we want to talk storage and padding- is where I'd hide the paraphernalia. (Which I totally wouldn't, TSA.)

We did have a secret (and totally scannable) weapon, however. It was known as The Christmas Elf Hat. Small, red, pointy, and ridiculously adorable on the miniature heat of a newborn, it forced goodwill upon people and imbued them with more than a little holiday spirit. (*We* think so, anyhow. I'm sure other passengers were all like, "Please shove over with your tiny gnome, I need to remove my laptop from the case".)

It brought on offers of help from folks in the terminal. Elicited coos from travel-weary attendants. *It even caused marauding Victorian carolers to stop and acknowledge her Christmassy awesomeness.*

I mean, sure, they were clearly planted there to be festive, but nowhere in their handbook did it say that they had to be extra nice to a baby. Nora inspired that, all on her own. Plus the hat.

We did hit one minor travel snag once we boarded the plane. The baby sling, which had been a safe and comfortable method of keeping my child quietly sleepy against me since those early days of Happy Hour screeching, was deemed unsafe for take-off. No one could adequately explain the reasoning behind this to me. I mean, sure, I had already purchased a Mrs.

T's and vodka from the flight attendant, but I was still able to hear reason. And they just didn't have it on their side.

Safety, they said. Nora would be safer on my lap and unrestrained. Right. Because nothing says Think Of The Children like an infant careening down the aisle at ten thousand feet. But I held her. And P.J. held my arms holding her.

And when no one was looking, we slipped her back into the sling and put a blanket over her head to hide the whole illegal action. Restrained *and* unable to breathe! (I think we know who got the last laugh here, Southwest.)

We traveled uneventfully like that for a good hour until Nora abruptly woke up and decided that she needed to nurse. Loudly and irately and more than immediately. So P.J. tried to help slide her out from the sling and under her blanket cocoon. Simultaneously, I attempted to discreetly free a boob from out of my nursing tank, which I had imagined would be an easy endeavor since the tank was under a nursing hoodie. Beneath a nursing blanket.

But all of those "easy access" items of clothing and coverage began to work against one another. A snap from the bra became entangled on the hoodie opening. The hoodie wouldn't stay where I had hiked it. And at one point, my boob was in very real danger of being shoved into a sleeve.

So much for attempting to privately and serenely feed my child. Nora, at this point, was completely enraged at the lengthy wait while her lunch was in the process of being freed. She decided to announce her complaints by thwacking at my tank, my hoodie, and the blanket. This had the unexpectedly mortifying effect of showcasing the very parts of my anatomy I had been obnoxiously covering with my all of my nursing gear.

Let's just say that it would have caused less of a stir had I just removed my entire outfit and fed the kid when she required it. Trying to do anything surreptitiously- and failing abysmally- is always way more obvious.

People pretended not to look, but oh, they looked. It's pretty hard to ignore a squalling child being comforted by a semi-topless woman. And when the woman's husband valiantly attempts to cover his wife with a billowing blanket? Well, that's just more of a sideshow to gawk at.

"THERE, THERE," P.J. yell-whispered at Nora. "SHH, I KNOW YOU'RE HUNGRY."

"IT'S OKAY, NORA," I begged of our purple time bomb. "HERE IS A BOOB. SHH."

The Christmas elf hat couldn't (or wouldn't) save us.

After that latest stint of public nudity, the usual bustle and stresses associated with Christmas and family didn't even register. In fact, nothing fazed me in the least. Just like at Thanksgiving, there was an abundance of arms to hold Nora and/or fix me some food.

I took multiple showers and guilt-free naps. Drank glasses

of wine in the presence of other people. (Whether or not they were also drinking was rather irrelevant. I mean, my family totally *was*, but the only thing that counted was the fact that I was not drinking alone.)

And while Nora slept on my brother in-law's shoulder, was being snuggled by my three sisters, had a bath courtesy of my Mom, was being handed toys/blankets/tiny socks by my nephews, or watched *The Three Stooges* with my Dad, I simply marveled at my lack of a to-do list.

The food, of which there has never been a shortage at my folks' house, was beyond plentiful and *totally taken care of, get out of the kitchen and go sit down, please.*

There was nothing for me to (think about attempting to) clean. In short, it was akin to my 4th grade summer vacation.

With wine.

I contemplated moving back home, and maybe even into my old bedroom. Or maybe even into one of the twins' rooms, as theirs were bigger.

On Christmas Eve, we all went to an early evening service and I prepared for the usual crush of families jam-packed into the church. The familiar carols that we've sung hundreds of times. And the sermon that would go largely unheard over the din of children excitedly shrieking and squeaking in their pews.

What I was *not* prepared for, however, was the intensity of my reaction to each and every moment of the mass. I found myself thinking about the Baby Jesus- and all babies, everywhere. All of them. Loved, unwanted, sick, wealthy, all of the babies. I thought of Mary giving birth in a manger. I was appropriately (and newly) horrified for her.

And I began to wonder if I had fully appreciated my cushy digs at Prentice, even with the night nurse that I was sure had been gunning for me. By the time that the lights were dimmed and candles lit for Silent Night, I was openly bawling (and unattractively snorting back my tears) while clutching a bewildered Nora to my clavicle.

Keep in mind, I'd been attending Christmas Eve services (among others) for three decades. But now that I had a baby (and post-baby hormones), it really struck a chord with me. It was easily the loveliest Christmas Eve I'd ever experienced.

It could've been the pre-church glass[es] of wine. Or I could've just had a truly spiritual moment, surrounded by family and friends in a house of worship.

That sounds a little nicer, so we'll go with that one.

CHAPTER FIFTEEN

(*Inequality.*)

And now, a random interlude/rant about the inequality of the interwebs.

For about a year and a half prior to our adventure, my blog had been an exercise in writing, a virtual scrapbook of my favorite unintentionally awkward advertisements, and a log of our unfettered, newlywed travails. I frequently (and surreptitiously) took cell phone shots of earnestly inscribed picture frames that paired up saccharine sentiments with inappropriate photography. Like, "My Soulmate, My Lover" etched around an image of a grandmother and her graduation cap-clad grandson. That got a lot of traffic. People love dime store hilarity.

A nice, supportive cross-section of people enjoyed my postings, and I was beyond thrilled to know that folks were reading them.

Then I had a kid. (Which, as everyone and their diaper brand now knows, really does Change Everything.) To be fair, suddenly there were more people than ever checking in on my writing. But now that Nora's chronicles were included on the site, this led to my classification as a Mommy Blog.

This did not strike me as particularly fair.

I was still writing with nary a through-line about our

rickety homestead, the thought process behind pajama jeans, my embarrassing love of belting Michael Bolton songs in my car, and the hilarity that is The Hamburgler, but add a few baby pictures and an anecdote about poop and boom: Mommy Blog. (Where were the Nomenclature Police earlier, when I would have *killed* to be termed a Hamburgler Blog?) The deeming of my stuff as now being "Mommy" bothered me for three distinct reasons:

For starters, the people bandying around the term "Mommy" to me had a hint of "isn't that cute" derisiveness in their voices and subject headers. And truly, there was really only a small cross-section of people who could actually get away with calling me Mommy. Chief among them was my own kid whom, by the time she got a blog of her own, I'd hope would upgrade my moniker to something slightly more grown up. Like "Mom", for instance. Or "Ace."

Secondly, I hadn't changed my style of writing. I was simply writing about whatever happened to be in front of my face on a daily basis. And sure, lately that included baby pictures and anecdotes about poop, but I would happily have blogged about a horse or a new lampshade if anyone bothered to make that my new day to day reality. But no, even with the addition of horse and lampshade, I'd still be tossed back in Mommyland at the first mention of teething.

And finally, people would never pull this diminutive crap with fathers. A man who writes about his life, his work, and the occasional changed diaper? *What a broadened world view from the modern father.* The nickname "Daddy" is still very much so ensconced in the world of "Sugar" or "Big," so even if "Daddy Blog" gets flung around, dudes still come off looking sexy and/or in charge. The blogs out there about fatherhood and stay-at-home Dads are considered edgy. Edgy! I'd give my right foot to be considered edgy.

(But then I'd probably just be called Eileen. Ba-da-bing! Maybe the Mommy Blog thing really isn't my only problem.)

I do realize that, for many, tossing this phraseology at Mothers Who Write On The Internet is harmless. But I will forever and ever Amen feel that shoving the word "Mommy" in front of the whole thing makes it really easy to discount the ramblings of an entire cross-section of women and their culturally relevant thoughts and opinions and occasional musings on Mayor McCheese.

Here's the rough part: I don't even have a witty alternative. Parent Blog sounds clinical. Or boring. (Boring is way worse than clinical.) Motherhood Blog sounds a little bit too "circle of life" for my tastes. I Know This Kid Who Happens To Live Here Because- Oh Yeah, She's Mine Blog is a bit too much of a mouthful. It's times like these when, yet again, The Hamburgler may actually be our best choice.

I'll even happily share all of the domain names I've snatched up. (And yes, I accept credit cards.)

CHAPTER SIXTEEN

(Workin' 9 to 5. Or 7:30 to 5. And then, if you include commuting time...)

Have I mentioned how lucky I was to have such a nice maternity leave? Are you surprised or concerned that so much happened during a theoretically "short" and restful" period of time? Have you contemplated calling Child Services on me yet?

While you mull over those questions, let's talk Post-Baby Leave.

I had never before really given much thought to the maternity leave laws in other countries, let alone in this one. But now that my own (terrifically long yet never long enough) leave's clock was just about up, I became intensely aware of just how many months Swedish mothers received. (Thirteen, for the record. *Thirteen!* That is even more than a year.) And don't even get me started on *paternity* leave for those forward-thinking, amazing furniture-engineering folks. I rallied for more time. I protested that our country didn't care about me as a person, let alone as a mother.

P.J. suggested that perhaps my quarrel was with him and not with the government, per se, as the good ol' U. S. of A. wasn't demanding my return to the world of nannying. I accused him of yet again changing the subject. And then I cried at him. Then I drowned my sorrows in nachos, guaranteeing a few more months in stretchy pants.

I had had close to ten weeks at home with Nora. The last two weeks were spent pointedly *not* looking at the clock, which works not very well at all. It's like the Just Waits were already having their win, except for the fact that I *wanted* to wait. I wanted to stay right there on the couch, wrapped up with my infant daughter and watching a marathon of infomercials and scrapbooking my baby's first two months of life. (Again, it must be noted: I *loved* my jobs nannying for two families and longtime friends. I seriously have no idea how people who have lukewarm feelings towards their jobs do it. I wonder if they fortify with nachos as well.)

My fluctuating hormones were still very much in play, as these thoughts of Sweden were usually hand in hand with a crying jag of decent length. Same goes for the decidedly cuddly and jubilant times. Sob City. I would also take a quick drive through Panic Town, wherein I imagined every single hardship that would befall my helpless child.

I would think about how there would be sadness on both of our parts when I wouldn't be able to immediately pick up Nora. I would think about an erratic activity schedule and nonexistent solo kid time. And I would think about how there would be a decided lack of couch naps. (I would think about that last one a lot.) But since uploading photo albums to Facebook doesn't exactly rake in the dough, it was back to earning a living for Nora n' me.

At that time, I was splitting my week between two families and their two children apiece. And while the transition to a nanny-with-infant probably wouldn't be butter smooth, it most likely wouldn't be like I had her strapped to my chest while cave spelunking. I realized that I'd be fortunate to have my child with me at all, and that some people would give their spelunking arm to spend as much time with their children.

That said, it completely grated whenever random folks would comment on how lucky I was to be able to go back to work with Nora, and- again- how much *fun* my day would be! No one likes being told that they're lucky. It ruins the serendipity of it all and slightly smacks of condescension. Being a nanny is a terrific (and frequently fun) job, and motherhood is easily my favorite non-interviewed position yet, but full-time childcare is rarely as whimsically cinchy as childless folks may think. Can you imagine if I went up to a paralegal and exclaimed "Law? What a *hoot!*"

Those same folks who deemed my job as "so fun and easy," (which was annoying hard to refute when I was covered in chalk and gummy snacks), were also in the same category who viewed nannies and babysitters as one and the same.

Which. They. Are. Not.

A babysitter comes over an hour before your pajama-clad kids go to bed, plays a game of checkers or Uno with them, takes the pizza money you left her, and watches whatever's on The WB while simultaneously texting her boyfriend until you return at 10:30pm.

A nanny (with or without infant) makes/finishes up breakfast, helps with homework *way* too advanced for her (why, New Math, *why?*), braids hair, finds the final puzzle piece under the cat's water bowl, convinces at least one person to go potty one more time (yes, even just sitting there counts), cuts so many crusts from sandwiches that a game of Jenga could be played with the remains, builds blanket tents that are equal parts safe padding and excitingly full of tunnels, cajoles naptimes (yes, even just lying there counts), takes over pick-ups, drop-offs, class participation and gluten-free snack preparation, reads every story with correct accents and intonation (and sometimes proper hand motions), bathes multiple children of varying ages and scrubbing abilities, and teaches the importance of modulation and killer hooks in select classic rock tunes.

Most of this happens before 1pm. (And yes, the majority of this stuff *is* fun. I'll totally admit it. But perhaps what I'm getting at is that we all need to stop talking at people? Can we all agree to just stop saying anything- positive or negative- in judgey tones? Yes?)

For the easily exhausted and not-overly-fond-of-children set, this job could be a death sentence. I'd always loved it, even when I returned home covered in multiple substances, the only identifiable one being glittery paste.

But I wasn't sure how it would jive once I added another kid to the mix (for instance, mine) and one who would automatically come in as the low [wo]man on the totem pole. If one of the kids in my (paid) care needed a bathroom, that need would automatically trump a fussy newborn. A hungry preschooler ranked above a teething infant. A five year-old's paper cut beat a baby's dirty diaper. In my mind, it was like a bizarre game of chess, and one in which Nora was already a low-ranking pawn.

My hormones clearly weren't letting up their maudlin melody any time soon, and I figured the actual work would be nicer than anything my melodramatic imagination feared. (Maybe even fun!)

To prepare Nora for Back To Work, I had planned out a whole sleep training regiment, cobbled together from various books and parents I respected. The weeks leading up to my return were spent convincing Nora that she wanted to nap by her lonesome in the bassinet. Maybe cry it out a little in her crib at night.

It totally worked, as she began sleeping all the way through the night really, really early on.

Or it didn't work at *all* since, as soon as I started nannying again, we were all really, really tired and would face-plant as soon as we entered our home each evening. I couldn't for the life of me tell you what *she* was doing in terms of restful sleep. Perhaps she was waking as frequently as newborns usually do in those early months, but totally gave up because her poor parents were completely unable to hear her through their log-sawing snores.

Which is *kinda* like sleep training. Through extreme negligence. Which I do not recommend. (Even though it totally works.)

I headed back to work in early January. It gets ridiculously cold in Chicago in January, especially early in the morning before the sun has even thought about fully getting up. I had to bundle my kid against the elements (which often included wind biting like teeth against exposed eyeballs) so I invented The Double Bear.

Nora *hated* The Double Bear. It consisted of being layered in her outfit, a thin fleece hoodie (complete with bear ears), and another, heavier coat (also featuring animal ears of some sort). She'd then be buckled into her car seat, which lived indoors during these early months for easier transportation. A light blanket for chewing would be tucked around her, and then the fleece car seat cover would be zipped up. Breathing was tricky. But this kid would never need fear frostbite.

I was completely terrified of forgetting something pivotal to our daily routines, so I over-packed for each day. By a lot. I even emailed and texted checklists and reminders to myself; fifteen diapers, a container of wipes and diaper rash cream, a swaddle blanket, a burp cloth, a smallish handmade quilt from my sister that doubled as a playmat, two changes of clothing, a portable rocking chair (with animal friends attachment bar) and at least three rattles in which Nora had, as yet, shown literally no interest. I also managed to bring one or two things for myself, like a wallet and a key or two. Walking into both homes with all that gear, plus the actual double-beared infant in her car seat, must have been a completely obnoxious sight.

"Here I am, ready to give your children and this day one thousand and two percent!"

Aside from the back-breaking amount of gear, there were other plusses and minuses of our new routine. Early morning nursing sessions before heading out for the day were quiet and snuggly moments of pure loveliness. Unfortunately, sometimes I'd have to wake her at 5:45am to get the ball rolling. (I hear the Experienced Mothers: Never wake a sleeping baby! *I know, right?*)

Nora also had a ton of exposure to ABCs and numbers really early on, but sometimes this was solely because letter blocks were being shoved directly into her eye socket by an overzealous toddler.

I did have plenty of opportunities to nurse my daughter, something that I was pretty happy about. Sure, sometimes these feeding sessions were accompanied by a toddler poking me and demanding "Is this a nipple? Is *this?*" At other times, I'd find myself carrying on a decently normal conversation with my employers while nursing Nora and cutting an English muffin into smaller bites for their child. Once, I even opened the door and signed for a UPS package with the kiddo attached to my boob. (Delivery confirmation, *indeed*.)

While I was proud of my ability to simultaneously adapt to a new schedule and keep my daughter sustained, I was slightly uncomfortable about borderline violating my rule of never been naked at work, ever.

The parents of these children were a wonderfully lenient bunch, and it just goes to show how much they valued me as a part of their kids' lives to let this sort of thing fly. As difficult as it sometimes was for me to drag Nora around town, I'm sure it wasn't their ideal childcare situation, either. I mean, here's this gal hefting an apartment's worth of baby supplies (plus an actual baby), constantly reassuring them that the quality of their kids' daily schedules would not be affected. (Squished, but not otherwise affected.)

An appropriate thank-you card has not been created for *this* type of scenario either, so I'll just use this space right here:

Thank you, families. I fully appreciate how you made adding one more yelling child to the mix seem, semi-nudity aside, perfectly normal.

Thank you, families, for being so kind. I had previously thought that your kindnesses knew no bounds, what with you having second children for whom I could care once your eldest children reached school age. That was especially kind. But then you topped it off by showering Nora with "just because" gifts. And setting up a room for her in your homes, complete with your own baby gear, Pack n' Plays, monitors, and toys.

Thank you for occasionally holding Nora so that I could go pee.

Thank you, not only for stocking the fridge with my favorite snacks and grownup meal items over the years, but eventually even having snacks and baby things for Nora on hand as well. (And you never, ever charged me for this, nor did you dock my pay even with the addition of another chomping human being coming into your house.)

And a big ol' thank you to you, families, for allowing me to tromp around your homes like a college kid on break; eating you out of house and home, doing loads of laundry, and leaving in a whirlwind of gear and rushed goodbyes.

Regardless of how many extra verses of *You Are My Sunshine* I taught your children, I know I can never fully repay you- especially since I charge *a lot*. Here's hoping, however, that I get the chance to try. (Maybe I'll watch your kids sometime?)

Nora adapted really easily to this new schedule and became a bit of a third child during the weekdays. After a month or two, she assumed that she'd just need to cry it out a little if someone was potty-training across the room. She realized early on that she wasn't the only game in town, and occasionally needed to entertain herself with the myriad of devices, attachments and toys I had brought with us.

Another point in her favor was how darned helpful she could be. For instance, if I had her slung in a carrier and needed to assist in teeth brushing, I'd just wait for her to yawn in full view of the kids; the "aww" it elicited was perfect for brushing back molars.

Even with my prior worries, the whole workforce thing went pretty smoothly. We became a large, well-oiled machine, or a carousel operated by an octopus. The only glitch came whenever someone needed to poop. I swear on a stack of bibles that, during that first month back, no one had a bowel movement as an isolated event. As soon as one of the older kids ran to the bathroom, at least one little kid would debate using their own potty (mid-"go"), and Nora would choose that moment to completely poop off her own diaper. This simulpooing happened at least once a day, catching me off guard each and every single time. It was like dodge ball. With poo. And I was always that kid against the wall who needed to change his pants and call his mother immediately after class. (No one with me, here?)

The big kids with whom we spent our days were an energetic and busy bunch- and they had the lessons and activities to prove it. Nora became a tagalong pal to things for which her own parents wouldn't otherwise have had the resources. She sat through her first ballet class at two months of age. Shortly thereafter came her first soccer practice. Then gymnastics, Spanish. Swimming. And twice-weekly preschool. There were playdates, museum trips, and a spin in every playlot park on Chicago's north side.

And Nora studied the kids in the way that really small babies often do, with eagle eyes and a monkey's mimic. I swear that she did things earlier because of them, too, like laughing, scooting, and refusing naps.

The thing that I was proudest of, however, was how quickly she picked up on baby sign language. This is another "thing" that parents from the old days roll their eyes at. *Why do you need to know what the baby is trying to say?* Back when I was a nanny sans daughter, I would assign myself certain tasks for each day. Something cool and ultimately helpful, like squeezing my hand and signing *milk, milk, milk* all day long to someone else's infant. (Other days it was how to draw the perfect chalk butterfly. I never said these were academically lofty goals.) Well, it paid off. The toddler at whom I *squoze, squoze, squoze* was now thrilled to sign at Nora's face all day long. Milk! More! All done! The trifecta of helpful baby signs.

Truth be told, I can't take credit for Nora's sign language since it was the positively chant-like repetition of a toddler and not Nora's exhausted Mom who drilled these words home. But, I *did* teach the toddler. (And you should totally see her chalk butterfly. Perfection.)

And sure, maybe parents don't necessarily need signs to know if their baby wants milk, more of something, or is all done. Sucking one someone's shoulder, screaming at the food bowl, and kicking the tray over are all decent indications of those things.

(Speaking of "not entirely necessary," I also added those wetness indicator strips on diapers to my running tally of obnoxious things. *How inept have we led manufacturers to believe that we are?* When I want to check if my kid is less than fresh, I do the ol' standby test of picking her up and actually smelling her diaper. But I *have* been known for my impressive scientific method.)

The benefits to Nora's social and intellectual skills more than made up for the fact that I still needed to wake her each time there was a big kid's school pickup or doctor's appointment. Unless it was blizzarding that morning. Or unless she had a slightly sniffly nose and I still had to drag her out of her crib. On days with detracting moments like that, the good/bad almost broke even. And there were definitely moments where I would glance over at Nora and just feel that day's bucket of goodwill slowly draining out of her. I would wonder if- maybe- she'd be better off with a nanny of her own, where she'd at least be the *numero uno* priority. Then I'd remember that nannies can't have nannies, because they'd just cancel each other out. Like *Time Cop*.

(Note: I've never actually seen *Time Cop*, but I like to think that the exact premise is nannies eradicating each other. Tangentially, I used to freely interchange *Time Cop* for *RoboCop*. That one's probably not about nannies eradicating each other, either.)

P.J. and I fell into the habit of driving to work together. I'd either drop him off or he'd accompany us to that day's house and then hop the train one or two stops more to his office. And it was nice on those early mornings; listening to the radio, sharing coffee and a cobbled together breakfast, apologizing to our daughter in the rear view mirror for whichever life choices led to us waking her each day, holding hands...

With P.J. dropped off, I'd gauge the day's car seat needs. And *boy*, did the Child Safety industry really clean up with the addition of seat restraints for bigger kids! Don't get me wrong, I'm all for a child sitting safely as opposed to sliding around in the back of a station wagon, but it's a serious money suck: The infant seat. The convertible car seat. The booster. And not only is it inadvisable for kids to sit in the front seat until the age of twelve, but these poor kids also have to endure the indignity of the backseat booster until they're 4'9". (My Nana would never have made the cut. Sorry, Nana, here's your booster.)

One of my favorite childhood photographs is of my Dad

driving a sweet red Porsche. My biggest and youngest sisters are in the backseat, and I'm in the front, holding my two year-old sister *on my lap*. I was nine. We were also about to embark on a (safe) speedy drive over a road we'd named Rollercoaster Hill.

Those were different times. You can tell, because at least one of us was un-ironically wearing a visor.

It would take roughly ten minutes to play Jenga with our impressive collection of borrowed child safety seats and decide how many to shove into the Passat. And as family-friendly as it was, we really stretched that poor car's capacity. Sometimes there was a convertible car seat or two. Most days a booster was squished next to Nora's infant carrier. It was almost an optical illusion each time I glanced into the rear view mirror. Forget a clown car; try a backseat full of kids aged two months to seven years.

While driving around one day with a carful of children, the oldest girl asked if perhaps I had ever given thought to a bigger car. The middle kid asked if it could perhaps have a backseat DVD player, because didn't I even *want* one? Nora was too busy attempting her third aborted nap of the day to chime in, but I bet she would've agreed with them.

And at school drop-off one morning, a kindly teacher suggested that it might be time to upgrade my family vehicle. I informed her that I didn't even *know* any of these children. (This, as it turns out, is not the most appropriate of childcare jokes.)

By the end of the workday, we were all pretty zonked. P.J. would meet us at either of the families' home and then we'd all drive back north to our neighborhood together. I'd hand him the keys and happily scoot over to the passenger side. This was fabulous for many reasons; family togetherness, a little bit of time out of the driver's seat for me, and- most importantly- it let Nora and me pass out for the commute and enjoy an uninterrupted nap. One time, P.J. left the two of us in the garage so we could sleep for a full hour. Blissful.

Once we were home for the evening, I got to be Just A Mom. (Which is kind of like saying Just The Pilot or Just The One With Keys To The House.) There, I got to be in charge of meals and cleanliness of the house and/or its occupants. Just like at work, only with less pay! The rewards, of course, were the moments of story time and snuggles that reminded me why I took on this job in the first place. The pros would outweigh the cons, and I'd try to keep these thankful moments in my heart each night.

Right before I'd pass out in a pool of someone else's spit up wearing ketchup-covered sweatpants on a night when no one had consumed anything even remotely dippable.

Nora, for all of her nuances, was a pretty easy baby. Besides napping like a pro (or at least playing possum like a pro), she was a superb eater. Around four months we introduced rice cereal. And she loved it. So we went on to serve wheat, oatmeal, and barley. Love, love, and love. Next up she tried smashed and strained peaches and almost ate the entire tray in her fervor. Then came all of the non-allergenic fruits and veggies and her own two fists. One time I served her some diced mangoes covered in rice cereal- for easier gripping, I had thought, but which in actuality just armed her with goopier projectiles. Torn up mini croissants from the neighborhood bodega. She straight up *craved* those, but we put the kibosh on croissants after discovering that, instead of chewing and swallowing, she was simply shoving each bite to the back of her throat, making her mouth into some sort of terrifying potato gun. (Also, there was a risk of choking.)

I marveled at this age. I knew from experience that the whole Eat Whatever I Put In Front Of You stage would be ridiculously fleeting, so I decided to make the most of it. And to tell you the truth, it kind of made me feel like a god. Nora would take a bite of something new, widen her eyes, and give me a look that seemed to say "I didn't *know* bananas were so squishy! Have avocados always been green? You simply *must* try this blueberry."

I had planned on going the jarred food route, but once I figured out how easy (and cheap) it was to make the majority of

Nora's food, I went gung-ho. I'd chop apples and boil them down for an hour: applesauce. Bake some sweet potatoes and butternut squash on a tray, let them cool, and boom: Orangey dinner. I'd steam or microwave peas and smash them up, sometimes using a hand-me-down baby food grinder that was seriously easier to operate than a fork and knife. Fruits and veggies would be blended together, sometimes I'd add a dash cinnamon or spices, and voila: instant baby-approved entrée. *I was now cooking food and keeping my child alive like a pioneer!*

Granted, I couldn't do this with all of her meals, as my grain-milling skills were rudimentary at best. But it paved the way for what I really wanted to be doing in the first place: just giving her portions of my dinner. This had the unexpected effect of influencing healthier eating habits for P.J. and me. We weren't exactly gonna shove some Hamburger Helper on our baby's tray, now were we? But that said, we certainly didn't smoothie all of her food by hand to feel lofty and if, say, someone had dropped off crates of strained pears onto our doorstep, that's most likely what our kid would've eaten. (Especially if they were those organic frozen cubes from Whole Foods. Those things look fantastic.)

Once I started sharing my dinner with Nora, I made her reciprocate and fork over some of her baby snacks. I found myself popping handfuls of puffed grains flavored with magical ingredients like pears and cherries. I'd tell P.J., "They're light as air!" (He'd tell me, "Stop eating the baby's expensive snacks!")

And as for those tiny little baby yogurts made from whole milk and manna from heaven, I'd like to lodge a formal complaint regarding their size. They're so wee that they can barely fit a grownup spoon. (I've heard.)

Come on, baby food manufacturers. You're making me look ridiculous.

Of course, once I re-entered the world of All Things Big Kid, Nora caught her completely expected first cold.

It made perfect sense. We spent our week with four children, all of whom had separate classrooms and activities. To properly gauge how many germs each kid was responsible for, I multiplied each kid's illnesses by thirty other kids (and their various wet sleeves), allowing for more than one activity or class per child. The number of potential germs was rather staggering. I should've spun her into a roll of anti-bacterial Saran Wrap. Super-resistant viruses and breathing risks be damned!

There's a certain type of bonding that goes down in the middle of the night with a sick child. Compounded with a new mother's feelings of ineptitude, it was particularly meaningful.

Suctioning improbably long boogies out of nostrils that have yet to form cartilage was a definite act of torture, regardless of the cheerfully tinny lullaby screeching out of the suctioning instrument. Steaming her in the small (master) bathroom within an inch of becoming a wonton caused her to look at me with more than a little disdain. And crying in a panic on the bathroom floor had nothing to do with methods of homeopathic care, but that happened too.

I spent way too much time worrying about whether or not to call the doctor. I didn't want him to think I was crazy or unfit, but I also didn't want Nora to suffer because of my pride. So we called him. A lot. And when he patiently asked us to describe her symptoms, we'd emote them to the nth degree: A fever? Nay, she's *on fire*. A rash? Sure, if a flesh-eating scaly plague can be categorized as a mere "rash." He told us we could give her some infant Tylenol to keep the fever down and then continue to steam and suction. We worried that, sight unseen, he was missing the very real possibility Nora had some new type of infant disease. A really bad one. We also scoffed at medicating her. We weren't *awful parents*.

These scornful thoughts lasted an hour. We then proceeded to dose her into oblivion. She may still be groggy by kindergarten.

Our first Daylight Savings and loss of an hour with a child was a real eye-opener, both literally and figuratively. This had never before bothered me, most likely because I am neither a farmer nor a Wiccan dependent on certain phases of the sun and the moon. (Full disclosure: I actually don't know upon what phases Wiccans depend.)

The time change affected Nora so strongly that you would've thought we'd begun waking her at 2am just to say hello. *She could not deal.* Even though we attempted to ease her into an adjusted nap schedule and a slightly earlier bedtime, she wouldn't have it. Obviously she had been charting the position of the sunlight on her walls (maybe *she's* a Wiccan?) and disliked her daily rhythms becoming topsy turvy. She became the equivalent of a foreign exchange student, sleepily murmuring "*Qué?!*" to us as she faceplanted at 5pm.

We forced extra sunlight onto our outdoors-averse child, made the room cavernously dark for bedtime, and prayed that this exhaustion would right itself by the time Fall Back rolled around.

The lack of sleep combined with worries over our daughter's potentially fried brain cells brought a new kind of Papa Bear in P.J. This manifested itself in a complete and utter inability to *just stand by* while neighborhood cars and car alarms (and neighbors) blared, beeped, and sounded off during awfully inappropriate hours. Like, past 9pm.

On more than one occasion I had to bodily prevent P.J. from going all *Gran Turino* on our stoop. (We can add that movie to the list of those which I've never actually seen. But from what I've gathered in the previews, P.J. screaming about someone getting the hell off his property would've fit into that screenplay quite nicely.)

And we were aware that neither the house's locale nor the neighborhood's character had changed much in the past year, but now that we had a sick child with a bassinet facing street traffic, it suddenly seemed like a downright unlivable place.

The car alarm *Carol Of The Bells* no longer seemed like the fun game of Neighborhood Watch that it had been only months earlier. (See? *Everything changes* once you have a child!) For starters, each alarm incited a rage directed at the car's owner. A cacophonous siren simply because a motorcycle passed by? Why does that idiot feel the need to protect a car that dumb?

"Give me a crowbar," I sleepily muttered to P.J. on more than one occasion. "I'll go finish the damn job myself."

With each outburst of ours, I'm pretty sure our neighbors collectively referred to us as The Angry Whiteys. This is fine.

As long as they said it to each other in quiet, conversational tones.

And Now, An Open Letter To My Daughter's First Best Friend:

Dear Doc Bullfrog,

You are a frog. A green-ish lovie from Carters, purchased by a family friend at Target, and are defined by your white on green polka dots and your embroidered proclamation that [You] Love Hugs! You were named after a great character in a lesser known Jim Henson film about an otter.

Speaking of otters, I did not plan on you. Nora's lovie was supposed to be a hard-won otter from Monterey. His name is Otto and I've Ugly Cried over him. And sure, he's there in the crib with you two, but he plays second fiddle to the glory that is your addictive scent.

At least I think you have an addictive scent. Why else would Nora have you plastered to her nose each morning, noon, and night? I'm trying to think of what the equivalent of crack would be to an infant, but since her other current addiction is needing to nurse half an hour before my alarm goes off each morning, I'm guessing you're better than mother's milk.

However, you are covered in dirt. And pee. More than a little spit-up. Cat hair, too! I wash you so often it's incredible that you haven't disintegrated into a pile of (huggable) green satin. And that rattle you've got, that shakey sound right in the middle of your noggin? The other day when pulling you out of the dryer, I noticed that your rattle sounded somewhat tinnier. I'm pretty sure that all of the repeated sanitizing of your little blankety body fused a part of your rattle brain to another part of your rattle brain.

Doc, when this realization hit me, I crumpled to the floor of the laundry room and *sobbed*. In that moment, I hated you. I despised how much my daughter adores you and how much wicked power you hold over me. You are the receptacle for a frightening amount of love in a staggeringly fragile body.

And there are no substitutes, either. Once I acknowledged that you might not survive until Nora's college years, I had both a childhood friend and my sister-in-law send me backup froggy versions of you. Three of the same frog, you ask? That's *ridiculous*. I know. It totally is. But, having only recently realized Nora's power to so fiercely love an object, I'm willing to do whatever it takes to protect this affection/ensure her feelings of security/get us out of the house without a two hour manhunt. So, three frogs it is. We named your backups Jacques and Brock, and Nora thinks they're quite nice. Great even. In fact, she likes to hold one of them up to you for a group snuggle. It's only when *you* disappear that things get real. When you're in the swim or are otherwise detained under the couch, they're interlopers. Insufficient comfort. *Terrible frogs.*

Listen, Doctor, since you're the only who'll do, we need to come to some sort of understanding. What say you agree to not snag on anything and require my subpar seamstress skills, and I'll try and ease up on the Stain Stick.

I love her, she loves you, so I guess I need to love you, too.

Respectfully,

Nora's Mom

CHAPTER SEVENTEEN

(Not for the faint of heart.)

I started to feel good about my ability to jive being a homeowner, mother, nanny, and mostly fully-realized adult.

So of course that's when our super helpful home reminded us that hubris is generally bad, choosing to time some eye-opening experiences during a period when our sleep-deprived eyes could barely open.

The house started this comeuppance on the tail end of a Can Do kind of week, and it began with the death of our trusty upstairs furnace. During the winter, in a city awfully close to a big ol' lake of negative temperatures, wind chills, and frozen tears.

Bizarrely and fortunately enough, our home still possessed two separately zoned heating sections. This meant that, instead of residing upstairs on the Ice Planet Hoth, we'd be able to sleep in the lower level's guest bedroom which was warmed by the new boiler. For its part, that contraption had recently decided to become The Little Engine That Could in terms of heat output.

Basically, when the heat was turned on for the main floor, the lower level was *really* on. And when the lower level's heat was turned off, that floor stayed decently warm for days but the upstairs instantly became Arctic. But barring our walk-in freezer of a converted attic on the third floor, this was our only valid option until we had the furnace fixed. So we stripped Nora down and prepared ourselves for a night on the surface of the sun.

There are few things like seeing your infant child sleeping in a portable crib, clad in only a diaper, and tucked into the corner of a boiling hot basement (because the upstairs of your home had *just broken*) to make you feel like perhaps you weren't super good at being a grownup.

(It might be interesting to note, however, that regardless of anything else going on in the house, the main floor's bathroom was independently icy. To the best of our knowledge, this was a direct result of that bathroom's vent being frozen into a permanently "open" position. No matter the heating or cooling attempts, the bathroom tile, walls, and fixtures were so cold that there was actually the danger of sticking to them like a tongue on a frozen pole. It was a lot like having an indoor outhouse, I imagine. Occasionally, one could feel whipping winds while showering. And again, this had nothing whatsoever to do with the temperature regulation on either floor (pole?), it was just a sadly concurrent bit o' awful that didn't even rank on the list of Things We Ought To Fix.)

Eventually, our heating and cooling guys showed up and quoted us six hundred bucks to repair the furnace. And yes, these were the ones who had repeatedly stolen our endcaps. We were desperate. But as a bonus, they already knew how special the inner workings of our house were. It saved us that awkward conversation. ("Your house is really weird." "I know.")

So it was either six hundred bucks for a fix, or pay over two grand to completely replace it, which it quite obviously needed. But, adding to our decision to go quick and easy was the knowledge (and additional cost) that, to get the furnace removed, a wall would have to be ripped out. Back when the third floor had been renovated in the eighties or thereabouts, a wall had been built clear around the old furnace, rendering it completely inaccessible except for a snaked hand. Obviously!

Here's something you never want to hear a contractor utter: "I don't even think they *make* this kind of furnace anymore!" (We fondly reminisced about hearing that exact phrase during the Time Traveling Boiler removal.)

We wanted heat. Eventually we wanted renovations. But we certainly weren't inclined to spend bank on a major tear-out of a relatively minor corner of the house. (That last part is a joke. Because it doesn't exist. Narwhals, leprechauns, minor corners of a house, all charmingly imaginary concepts.)

So we opted for the slightly cheaper option, telling ourselves that we'd deal with a complete overhaul when we decided to go ahead with our plans for installing heating and cooling vents throughout the house. (Yeah! And then we'd seal the deal for our indoor pool, ballroom, and regulation size soccer field!)

Our plumber told us that the part we needed would be in "within the week" which, in Plumber Speak, could mean anytime between an hour from now and the summer solstice. I knew that we couldn't possibly spend another night in our subterranean desert, since I had actually gasped myself awake and yelled at P.J. for breathing all of my air. So I rearranged the contents of my office on the second floor and prepared to make it fit for a baby.

I spent that whole day reprioritizing outlet space and trying to find enough floor space for a Pack n' Play to successfully not be buried under stacks of paper. I also spent a good chunk of this time wondering why it was that a writer needed an "office" that contained a bed, a bench, piles of laundry needing buttons or repairs, all of the books deemed too embarrassing for display, and enough knick knacks to open a gift shop.

I didn't, however, question why every personal diary from 1985 onward needed to be stacked in chronological order under a bench- that had seemed obvious. (Reference!)

Three hours after I finished this hefty sorting/stacking/shoving project, the plumber called to tell me he'd found The Piece and would be over in a jiffy. Which is also a nebulous Plumber Speak word; but this time he meant it. Thus, our bedrooms were nicely heated by the time I moved Nora's belongings for the third time in twenty four hours. This, of course, rendered my afternoon's organization (on my "day off," no less) completely and utterly useless. Except for the fact that my office's junk was now stacked even more neatly in case anyone ever had a hankering to hem some pants.

Later that month, we noticed a smell coming from Nora's nursery. An hour spent on hands and knees sniffing various corners of a baby's bedroom (a game that no one wins), made me more determined than ever that something was amiss, perhaps something of a gassy nature. F.J., for his part, was certain it was just residual stink from Nora's diapers (further proof that even my husband questioned my housekeeping abilities).

He left for work and I called the gas company, ready to rule out that li'l possibility. The extremely helpful gal on the phone informed me that someone would be there within ten minutes. I was rather impressed by this turn of events; none of our contractors even returned our *calls* within ten minutes.

A large, gruff man immediately showed up and made quick work of waving a sensor around Nora's room. The thing lit up like the Fourth of July.

"Yup," he told me. "Gas leaks. In at least four spots that I can pick up on here."

I felt momentarily vindicated; something *was* wrong and I was right! About three seconds later his words registered. Gas leaks? In the kid's room? Why did *that* get to be the thing I had to be right about? He went downstairs to our boiler and found leaks leading up to it, as well as in the pipes lining our laundry room's ceiling. He told me it was "bad." I nodded like I had any idea what t-pipes and soldering junctions meant.

I then waited for the part that I usually liked; how he was going to fix it by the end of the day. Preferably for less than that week's grocery bill.

I was sorely disappointed.

"Gotta turn it off. Law."

"Gotta turn *what* off?" I asked. "Surely you don't mean my sole means of warmth and food preparation, do you? When I have a newborn and two cats and a woman ill-prepared for inclement weather residing in this house at this very second? Because it's *winter*?"

He shrugged.

"Law."

He went on to tell me to tell My Guy to rip out this wall *here* and search for the piece that…*there*…and if that didn't do it (which it probably wouldn't,) to think about running a line across *that*. It might involve the tearing out of another wall.

Right about then I began to panic; at the overload of information, the very possibility that Nora would freeze to death in the room I had so lovingly rid of maroon paint, and the notion that this entire thing was my fault for having called in the first place.

Voice quivering (and hating myself for it), I asked the man to write down everything he had just told me. He responded that it was too much to write, and that I should just use my *eyes* and *ears* and remember what to tell My Husband.

And that's when I began to cry. But it was the kind of cry that one tries really hard to tamp down, resulting in a truly unattractive squeaking. The kind of weeping that comes from being treated like the Little Woman; and actually furthers every bad stereotype known to [wo]man.

He shut off the gas. I even thanked him. (Manners are everything.) He left and I stared at Nora for a good few moments, unsure as to what the heck just happened. But I had a niggling suspicion that perhaps I should act.

So I called P.J.

It took a good moment or two for him to realize it was me on the other end and not some bizarrely hyperventilating squirrel. (He even kindly allowed for a few uncomfortable and confused moments where I just sobbed loudly.) He responded in true P.J. form, telling me He'd Take Care Of It.

Having left work early, he contacted Our Guy (actually a new and slightly more expensive Guy, but we were quickly losing faith in our Other Guys) and explained the urgency of the situation to him. And bless both of them; they were there within the hour.

The New Guy found and fixed the leaks without having to rip out any walls; at least upstairs. Down in the laundry room with the boiler was another, more complicated story, but he took care of it. I'm pretty sure it involved t-pipes, whatever the heck those magical things are.

This whole endeavor took about seven hours and a thousand dollars, but things were eventually plugged and sealed and re-routed. And even though it was now well into the evening hours, People's Gas sent over another person to check things out and turn 'em back on.

The next hour involved more than a little male strutting and competition between Our Guy and the People's Gas' Guy as they checked each other's work. (P.J., not wanting to be left out, offered up some opinions on pipes; T or otherwise.) The People's Gas Guy was being a complete jerk, and I felt bad for Our Guy. Still, I wanted Our Guy to give in; I was totally afraid that the People's Gas Guy would storm off in a huff and leave us without heat. (Men.) So I soothed the egos of everyone involved and restated how *amazing* they all were, and how *useless* I would have been without each and every one of them. (Heavy-handed? Sure. But I really wanted heat back in the house.) And it's painfully true; had none of them showed, I would still be sitting on a chair and fluttering my hands in a panic. Maybe to this day.

If homeownership has taught me anything, it's that being The Little Lady can sometimes just get the job done.

Thankfully, the whole shebang was taken care of in only one day, one of the few times we could claim such a thing in this abode. We still strongly recommended that Nora not light matches in her room, what with the possibility of residual gas. And, you know, the whole "being a baby" thing.

And say what you will (and we have) about this place, but even after a day sans heat, the brick construction kept the inside temperature from dropping below sixty degrees. Not too shabby, considering it was a balmy twenty degrees outside that day. Those three little pigs were really onto something.

Then again, I've heard that haunted houses have a sort of weird thermal energy, so that's probably it as well.

To continue playing our fairly expensive game of Whack-A-Mole, our lower level still had an elusive bad smell. I had initially chalked it up to the house's haunted nature. P.J. had wondered if there was a body in the walls. (Both possibilities had equal chances of being true.)

Our latest plumber was definitely rather expensive. However, since we were fairly certain that he was not a kleptomaniac, we were inclined to pay a little more this go-round.

He suggested that our lower level bathroom might be the cause of some of the house's problems. As it turns out, it wasn't necessarily the root of the smell, but it was indeed *a* problem. We discovered that one of the home's previous owners had renovated the basement apartment's bathroom and, after digging up the concrete foundation, placed a new tub directly on the exposed dirt floor.

Adding to the list of things that I am *not*, is a builder. But to place anything on plain dirt seems sloppy at best. Dangerous (and gross) at worst. So we added another contractor to our growing collection and he removed the rusted out tub. When they lifted the thing out, however, they discovered an intricate system of tunnels that would have made the Incas proud.

But they weren't intended for any ancient civilization. Instead, they were home to the worst of my irrational fears: rats.

We called in the first of our exterminators. He assured us that, while there was Definite Rodent Evidence, there were no *recent* traces of the vile things.

The contractors sealed up the tunnels and completed work on a gorgeous new soaking tub, finishing it all off with sparkling new tiles. (Hey, if the thing had to be replaced, might as well make it *slightly* worth our while.) We were thrilled with the new look. We were stoked that it was over, and so easily, too!

And we were alarmed by the frantic scratching that mysteriously appeared and vanished near the stairwell and, oddly enough, our front living room.

So we did as any new parents with overwhelming home issues would do: we ignored the potentially alarming sounds. We'd gotten awfully good at Playing Possum since signing away our lives. I'd also taken on the role of Sloth, falling immediately asleep at the first signs of stress. Some might suggest that this was neither the best nor the most adult way of dealing, but on the plus side, I'd never in my life been more sporadically rested.

If you didn't count the mile that I jumped every single time the walls made noise, you could say that we lived in a blissful state of ignorance. A short-lived one.

A few days after we had installed the new tub (and ignored some wall-scratchings), I left the house to run some quick errands and enjoy the freedom of flapping my unencumbered arms about. In the midst of this jaunt I received a phone call from P.J., who calmly and quietly informed me that he had just seen something. When pressed, he admitted that it was a smallish butt scurrying under the kitchen stove.

A rat butt.

Even though I was in the relative security of our neighborhood Walgreens, I screamed.

By the time I got home, P.J. was thoroughly "on it." He was holding Nora up higher than was probably necessary with one arm and brandishing a gigantic grill spatula with the other. I promptly took our child and proceeded to climb a chair to become the woman in the *Tom & Jerry* cartoons.

Nothing happened.

We called the exterminator, who deemed the situation Not An Emergency, as rats do not climb stairs or come out into the light. (We called the second of our exterminators.)

Tentatively going about our night and getting Nora ready for bed, I ran back into the kitchen briefly.

And saw the rat.

Skulking (as rats do) on the other side of the kitchen. In the light. With people around. (This was obviously a rat who did not care about what certain exterminators thought of his daily habits.) I screamed again and the beastie hightailed it back under the stove. P.J., wisely determining what had occurred, was at my side in record time.

He told me *he'd handle it.*

I jumped up on a couple of moving boxes and proceeded to watch things unfold from between my fingertip-covered face. (Also, are you confused as to why our home still possessed unpacked storage boxes? Discuss.)

P.J. rolled up an old beach towel (the apex of home security systems), and wadded it under the stove to buy him some time. (Few things are as widely respected in the animal kingdom as rolled terrycloth.) Then he got his gear ready; some glue traps, the grilling tongs to go with the large spatula, a broom, some heavy work gloves, and some outer wear.

We heard more scritch scratches, this time from under the kitchen sink cabinet. We determined that this thing must be a) half-starved, b) crazy, and/or c) not afraid of us at *all* to keep resurfacing while we were still in the room. (We also wondered how he was now under the sink. Was there a monorail behind our kitchen walls?)

The cabinet door began to press outward slightly, closing back in on itself. This led us to scream out loud *and* thank God that we had prematurely installed child-proofing on our cabinet doors.

Since I kept on screaming, P.J. had no choice but to be the stoic adult in the situation, though I imagine this wasn't his ideal Sunday evening, either. (Not to mention the rat's night. I'm sure it was the rat's worst evening ever.)

The thunking behind the cabinet doors led us [P.J.] to believe that the glue traps had worked, so we [he] gingerly poked the door open to see a thoroughly cheesed-off rat wearing oversized glue trap galoshes.

Wildlife tip: glue traps are for mice. Anything less than a cannonball for a rat will just piss him off and make him stronger.

Now, the rest of the story is secondhand, as my daring husband instructed me to leave the room. Because- again- he would *handle it.*

In a nutshell, it happened like this: P.J., clad in heavy clothes and heavier gloves, spent an hour attempting to sweep the positively irate glue-booted rat into a paper bag. Eventually, he was successful. (Although P.J. says that my shrieks were distracting, I like to think that the adrenaline was akin to that of a sporting match.) He then grabbed the tongs and carted this dog n' pony show outside to the alley.

I don't know what went down out there. P.J. says we

never need to speak of it again. Whether that means he Godfathered him or shipped him off to charm school, matters not to me. What happens in the Kedzie alley stays in the Kedzie alley.

And if I had looked upon P.J. with a new light in my eyes after the birth of our child, now I *really* saw him as my knight in household armor. Especially after he reached under the stove and unrolled the beach towel to find a tooth-bitten hole the size of a tugboat.

I still found myself nostalgic for the days when we feared the house to be haunted. And it was still my go-to explanation every time something freaky happened in the home.

Bathroom heating vent falling on my head in the shower? Ghosts. (Ticked off ghosts who didn't care for the Desert Sand color which I had recently painted that room.)

Smelling a new men's aftershave in the hallway? Attractively scented ghosts. (Later debunked as a new eucalyptus AirWick, but *come on*, who changes someone's air freshener without a discussion or warning?)

Or when the doorbell rings off and on for hours *with nary a person at the front or side doors?* Ghosts. Annoying, naptime ghosts. And sure, that one turned out to be an extra doorbell attachment that kept shifting in the downstairs junk drawer, setting off its outside counterparts. (But who was shifting the contents of the junk drawer? That was *my* question.)

I got in the habit of apologizing to the room whenever something unexplained occurred. George, the previous owner whom I also believed to be our Ghost in Residence, was generally the recipient of my contriteness. Then I'd get freaked out about conversing with a ghost, so I'd hop into bed and pull the sheet up over my ear (another effective home and personal safety method).

It wasn't like we needed any help in upping our home's stress levels. I was doing just fine and dandy on that front all by my lonesome.

During the bathroom renovation, we remembered that one of our side door's locks was strictly decorative. As in, we didn't have a key. The realtors didn't have a key. (Nor, I imagine, did the squatters.)

So why on Earth would we keep a doorknob without any method of securing or unlocking it? Well, since the rest of that doorframe had been a jumble of boarded up parts and stapled plastic, it was easily the nicest thing on that part of the house. We viewed it as a sign that we hadn't bought *the* most derelict property on the market. It had a shiny bronze doorknob!

We informed all guests and contractors about this quirk, and it generally went without incident. Unfortunately, the Serbian contractors who had fixed up the tub and tile so nicely (and who locked up when they were done with the day's work) weren't exceptional at remembering that nugget of knowledge.

(To be fair, it *did* come in a far second to correctly remembering which rat holes to plug up. So if I had to choose my battles…)

So, one Monday evening in frigid February, Nora and I returned home a little early from work and I settled her into the family room's Pack n' Play for a quick change. I had been feeling so good at my abilities to balance work, baby, and household, that I jaunted out to get the mail; this was usually P.J.'s job at the end of the day. Wouldn't *he* be surprised? I was being downright Donna Reed, what with my ability to keep our child alive, think about starting supper, *and* fetch the mail.

The buzz from my pride kept me so warm that I ran outside in a shirt and yoga pants, even though it had recently started snowing. As I pulled the door shut behind myself, it occurred to me that I hadn't brought a key. No matter, I decided. I didn't have to lock up for the seven steps to the mailbox. (But I kept a fierce Eagle Eye out. No one would sneak in behind me and kidnap my child, no sir.)

Mail under my arm, I walked back and turned the doorknob. It was locked. It took a moment to realize what had happened. (My first thought, naturally, was *ghosts*. Damn them!) I couldn't figure out how I had exited a locked door; then I remembered. When the bronze knob was locked, it still turned from the inside, appearing not locked at all. (How delightfully weird!) No problem, I thought. I would just enter from the front door, where Nora and I had come in immediately after work. Then I remembered that I had locked that one behind us after getting inside; for neighborhood safety, of course. So now I was now stuck outside in the frigid Chicago evening, bare arms exposed. And then Nora began to cry.

I began to wish for a lock pick or side alley intruder. Maybe one of our ghosts. (Where are you *now*, George?)

Since I was without keys, cell phone, or jacket, I'll admit that I felt a little frozen (and not just from the snow) and spent a few moments just staring at the locked door without a single thought in my head. After about five minutes, I realized that the knob was remaining locked, and it didn't look like anyone was going to help me out any time soon. I knew that P.J. arrived home between 5:45 and 6:30 on days where he didn't carpool with us, but I had no idea what time it currently was. My brain was telling me to go get help (like Lassie!), but I knew for a fact that our neighbors would *not* help us, let alone answer the door. Besides, I couldn't possibly leave Nora stranded in the safe, warm house in the relative comfort of a crib.

So I stood outside the door for a good twenty minutes. Because, as anyone knows, standing in the proximity of a screaming baby is better than "leaving" her. Hearing her distress but standing my ground felt like penance. As a newly converted Catholic, this comforted me slightly.

Eventually, I had to leave. My arms were turning blue. I bolted up the street to the Colombian grill (the same one whose non-stop chicken rotisserie festival had previously nauseated my pregnant self) and begged to use their phone. They thought I was insane. I *looked* insane. Finally, one server let me use his cell phone to call my husband. I left messages on his work line and cell as he didn't pick up either line. Thoughts ran through my head: what if P.J. was working late? Or stuck in transit? Or had gotten a drink with friends (the jerk)?

The kindly waiter offered me a warm beverage, another phone call, a sweatshirt; but I had to go back to my post at the side alley tundra.

Nora was now wailing. And as I embody many types of "crier" (among them sympathetic, guilty, and a self-pitying crier), I wept along with her. My arms were now stabby pieces of meat, my eyes were blurring, and I was sure that someone had phoned Child Services on me. (Maybe they'd bring a locksmith?)

About three hundred hours later, a frantic P.J. rushed through the gate and up the front steps to the door (the one which possessed no such decorative lock). He bolted down the stairs to his baby and spent half an hour cooing and cuddling her, reassuring her of his love.

I lamely announced that I had gotten the mail. And had pulled out a frying pan for dinner. Nora glanced up at me from her father's arms, and- *I kid you not*- pointedly looked away.

It was agreed upon that a lengthy, boiling hot shower was the answer. Plus, it would mask my newly rehydrated tears quite nicely. I also decided then and there to *never again* make that God-awful sojourn to the mailbox.

EPILOGUE

(I think we've learned something. For starters, we should all be renting.)

I wish I could say that our Big Year ended on some sort of glorious moment of self-reflection, but no, it was locking myself out of our home that marked twelve months of this adventure. Some people have big years that consist of starting a vineyard in a ramshackle part of Napa or journaling on parchment as they sail to the Greek Isles. Not me. I discover I'm pregnant during a Mario Kart-off, buy a questionable house in an even more questionable part of town, and proceed to discover that not one single thing I learned in my twenties had any helpful application during the 2009-2010 fiscal year.

But aren't I lucky? Because the fun didn't end there. If I'm fortunate enough to live to 100 (and Nora is healthily 29 years behind me), I'll *still* have moments of utter stupidity and brilliance and awe regarding my kid and this wonderfully stupid house.

I did learn some useful stuff during and after that year, however. And here's a big one, which I will now impart to you and probably break some sort of Parent Code: When I complain about how tough my new life can be, how exhausted P.J. and I are, and how much we miss our carefree days...

...Sometimes I'm lying.

It's true. Sure, any job is tiring, and there are definitely days where I want to hop on the nearest express bus, take it to the closest lakefront beach and Just. Keep. Walking. But prior to all of this, I had no idea how gorgeous a Sunday morning at home could be with a kid. Coffee on the couch, the paper already pre-sorted into important piles (Parade Magazine, the comics, and any of the Sunday inserts for me, anything actually informational for P.J.), a snuggly baby being passed back in forth, and nary a hangover between the three of us.

I don't really miss events at bars. I tell people I do, but I'm playing it up for their sake. If I never again pay eight bucks for a vodka tonic, it'll be too soon.

And even though my kid is usually covered in some sort of unmentionable substance, here's another secret: I think she smells awesome. I can't explain this one either, but the sweet baby breath makes everything my child holds and uses smell like a fragrant blend of fleeting and innocent infancy. (Diapers are exempt from this, but easily cleaned so we can return to what my kid actually smells like.)

A few people I know are certain that I've completely Stepforded myself, but here's another truth bomb: Even when I'm distinctly *un*happy, the new low still surpasses what used to be the old neutral. (I was shocked, too.) When I first had Nora, I so badly wanted to stay home with her full time and not have that choice completely drain our savings and cost us our house. Two and a half years ago, I got that dream job. (I also began writing freelance articles, including one review comparing and contrasting backyard tiki torches- so don't even try to tell me that dreams don't come true.)

Boredom is never an issue with our daily lives. I get asked that a lot, "Aren't you *stir-crazy*? What do you *do* all day?" And the answer is: Everything. And nothing. There are few things that require you to be more in the moment than an infant. Add a toddler or a school-aged kid to that mix, and you've got a nonstop parade of demands, wonderment, and glitter. (Maybe *that's* why I don't miss my performing days.) This ability to have such one on one time with my silly and positively edible offspring blisses me out, so I'm always amazed when people are dismissive or derisive about stay-at-home parents (and I have been since I was a child-free nanny). Because whether or not it's your cup of tea, it's *work*. Important work. (Exhausting work.)

What do I do all day? Patching baseboards aside, I'm raising patrons of the arts. (Respectful) war protestors. Barefoot hippies (if my husband has his way). Classic rock nerds (if I have mine). Intelligent, creative, and kind global citizens. In short, I'm in charge of shaping good people.

I think our society needs that just as much as we need doctors and coffee harvesters, don't you?

So what if I've completely given up the ability to go out at the drop of a hat or have grownup conversation before bedtime? Besides post-bath snuggles and the thousandth reading of *Goodnight, Moon*, what was so great about the hours of 5 to 8pm, anyhow?

As for this house; well, even when I wrote the first page I knew that there wouldn't be a *There, It's Done* chapter. No final renovation and *a ha* moment where we were finished working on this house forever and ever. I'm beginning to realize that the people who proclaim how Houses Are Never Done may actually be right. (As long as they don't tell the Just Waits, I think I can live with that small allowance of martyrdom.)

Within the last few years, the following events transpired:

The upside-down insulation on the crawlspaces was removed, and right-side up insulation was added. I'd like to say that we were driven to do this project because of the savings we'd reap each winter, but no. The true impetus was the knowledge that, just behind the crawlspace doors, poorly installed insulation proclaimed THIS SIDE FACES ROOF and quite visibly, too. It made me twitch. It was also discovered that the attic crawlspace directly above the kitchen housed uncovered track lighting wires, just hanging out in the loose insulation. This concerned us.

The entirety of the electrical system was brought up to code. Apparently, back in the day, live wires were wrapped in paper and cloth and no one worried one whit about it. During this project, the breaker boxes were converted into one single family unit, as opposed to the three-flat that the city so dearly wanted to tax us for. The silver lining to the exorbitant electrical overhaul expense was that I got a sweet dimmer in both the living and dining rooms. Now we could be poor in romantic lighting.

The lower level second kitchen was completely gutted. (That poor room.) During a routine removal of the downstairs countertop (as you do), P.J. and my oldest sister found something awful. Behind the counter island was a ton of concrete and behind *that* was a truckload of water damage and mold. And when we brought in the experts to check out the surrounding walls, they discovered more of the same. For about two weeks after that we had walls ripped open to the studs from the windows to the foundation. Mold remediation occurred. New drywall was brought in. And then I painted it Spring Green.

The main floor bathroom- the one that was forever freezing cold- was hiding an unfortunate secret. During a routine unclogging of the sink, our plumber agreed that yes, absolutely, there was a lot of hair in the sink. But perhaps what was causing even more of an issue was the fact that water couldn't properly drain, *as the sink pipe had never been secured into the wall*. It was just sort of resting into a vaguely dug out hole. And while this was being taken care of, they noticed a slow leak coming from the base of the toilet. No big deal, they said, so they removed the seal- only to find that the toilet had never been secured either, and hung out at a slight angle. The leak was due to the fact that the base had been improperly balanced on the *two layers of* tile that a previous owner hadn't felt like fully removing. The toilet was basically a tenuously connected, tipsy chair. (And this finished room had been a *gold star* during our tour!)

And the mother of all abode abominations: our sewer pipe collapsed. During the subsequent six and a half weeks of daily plumbing crews, demolition crews, and renovation crews, (not to mention therapy crews), they found cesspools under the lower level bathroom (the one of Rat Narnia/Brand-New Bathtub fame, proving that even when you're done with a room, you're still never done). Sewage pipes were found to be connected to nothing at all. Plumbing fixtures hung loose and unaffixed to any wall or floor. Cross beams in the bathroom's ceiling had been cut into willy nilly, the kind of beams that *support the actual house*. The entirety of the lower level was gutted and multiple rooms were taken down to the studs; including, of course, the ever-suffering and recently renovated second kitchen. This was the project that tested me the most as a homeowner and even as a mother. (This was also the project that firmly cemented my belief in ghosts. Angry, spiteful, get-out-of-my-house ghosts.) I found that I did *not* do well with daily jackhammering, daily cleaning of concrete dust, dirt, and sewage, daily visits from foremen and contractors and insurance agents, and daily crying over my babies' heads.

Yep, babies. That's another project worth mentioning. Two years after Nora, we had our second child, a sunbeam of a gal named Susannah Mae- who turned into a monkey of a kid. We had so much fun with her that we made it a trilogy with the addition of Jasper Callahan in December of 2013. (I'm not going to lie and say it wasn't fantastic to finally use the boy named we had picked out as Nora's alternate. Because it was. After five years, *someone* living here was getting named Jasper.)

So this home has yielded some pretty good projects, too.

I hold onto thoughts like that when, for example, the newly christened "girls' room" begins raining down powdered insulation from the disintegrating acoustic ceiling tiles…

This work in progress still has elements we can't stand, features stuff we're inordinately proud of, and hosts more than one shrieking nudie sprinting around in a towel. We now have some neighbors we love dearly, and whom we cling to in a completely *non-psychotic/ best friends forever/ thank you for grabbing my mail* way. There's usually a drunken and shirtless poker game going on two doors down all throughout the day and night. And our front stoop still sees more than its fair share of others' bodily functions. But recently, one of the drunks next door stopped by with a *horchata* for P.J. His *vecino*. We were touched. (We didn't drink it, but we were touched.)

And I'll tell you this much: I couldn't have picked a better guy with whom to make up all of this grownup nonsense. Even when every single thing goes wrong, P.J. will still agree with me one hundred percent that it's *everyone else* who's insane. (Not us. Never us.) We look at each other with our thumbtacked house and our questionably clad, marvelously noisy children- and we realize that there's nowhere else we'd rather be.

I'm pretty sure that means we're home.

Acknowledgements

As clichéd as it is to thank one's parents, I have to thank my folks Deb and Dave Flynn for duct-taping this thing together with us. Quite literally, we couldn't have done it without you. Thanks for everything up to and including the steadfast knowledge that I'd cobble a book together someday…and that I'd be a good person, despite lacking in the "mathly" realms.

Thanks to P.J.'s Dad Mike Schoeny for moving us in, to his Mom Natalie for furnishing us along the way- and to both for raising this ridiculously wonderful guy with whom I get to share a mortgage.

To my sisters Kate Grant, Rachel Flynn, and Emily Flynn (and bros Tom Grant and Dan Pesquera) for so, so many things. Things we don't even have room for here. But I'll just say thank you for always making me feel like a great writer- and the funniest one in the family. 'Cause now it's in print.

I owe my youngest sister Emily a huge debt of gratitude for that ridiculously wonderful map on the inside cover. My sister in-law Dorrie McCarthy's graphic design skills are second to none, as evidenced by the classy book jacket. And if I'm ever in a pinch? Greta Funk will always hook me up with stock photos.

Much love to Lily, Julia, Jen & Jeff Seaver; Peyton, Lucas, Molly & Kerry Prout; and Maeve, Declan, Jack Finn, Michele & Brendan Peterson: Thank you so much for allowing me to take care of your families (while treating me like one of your own).

Thanks to my wonderful Auntie Joan (Updike Martin!), for keeping me in the lemonade and enchiladas.

Hugs and high-fives to J. Wilder Konschak and Matt Cronin for early draft edits, unsentimental critiques, and gentle grammatical reminders.

To Billie Diamond, our terrific realtor- even though she's *still* shaking her head at us.

To Annie Gloyn, Kathryn Daniels, Bethany Hart, Hubbell Radue, Josh Samuels, Stephanie Crowell, John Ryan, Andy Hager, Kris Simmons, and Helen Lattyak: if not for you guys, absolutely zero things would've been painted, shoved, packed, or spackled. (I love you.)

Natalie Rothgeb, your Pilates sessions made me the svelte, leggy goddess I am today.

Thanks can't even cover what's owed to the ladies of DBA: you know who you are, what you do, and exactly what needs to be said at all times. I love you from the bottom of all my parts.

There's a core group of lovelies who've been faithfully reading Lollygag Blog since its shaky inception in June of 2008. Again, you know who you are (and *I* know who you are) and I hope you know how deeply grateful I've always been.

Nora, Susannah & Jasper: You guys made me a Mom, and I'll forever be grateful. I love you three more than morning coffee and pancake Saturdays.

And to P.J.: I'm not going to keep telling you how great you are. This is getting ridiculous.

*

Visit www.lollygagblog.com for more of this kind of thing.